HEAL YOUR LIVING

The Joy of Mindfulness, Sustainability, Minimalism, and Wellness

YOUHEUM SON

PARALLAX PRESS
BERKELEY, CALIFORNIA

PARALLAX PRESS

2236B Sixth Street
Berkeley, California 94710
www.parallax.org

Parallax Press is the publishing division of Plum Village
Community of Engaged Buddhism, Inc.

Cover and text design by Heesang Lee

ISBN: 978-1-952692-15-4

Library of Congress Cataloging-in-Publication Data

Names: Son, Youheum, author.

Title: Heal your living : the joy of mindfulness, sustainability, minimalism, and
wellness / Youheum Son.

Description: Berkeley, California : Parallax Press, 2022

Identifiers: LCCN 2021061301 (print) | LCCN 2021061302 (ebook) | ISBN
9781952692154 (paperback) | ISBN 9781952692161 (ebook)

Subjects: LCSH: Mindfulness (Psychology) | Well-being. | Mental health.

Classification: LCC BF637.M56 S73 2022 (print) | LCC BF637.M56 (ebook) |
DDC 158.1/3--dc23/eng/20211220

LC record available at https://lccn.loc.gov/2021061301

LC ebook record available at https://lccn.loc.gov/2021061302

1 2 3 4 5 / 26 25 24 23 22 21

MESSAGE OF GRATITUDE

I bow in and send my lotus prayer to fellow practitioners
and friends within our community. It is truly a gift to arrive here
as a guide and student standing side by side.

I also send deep gratitude to my teachers for all their wisdom
and generous offerings. It is a blessing to be a student of
Thich Nhat Hanh and to continuously learn valuable insights
from Neville Goddard and Helen Schucman.

May I reach those in need by sharing what I have learned
and keep incorporating within my daily practice. I wish to
give back by being of benefit to those who have generously
given. I continue with my own life as my message,
each and every step, each and every breath.

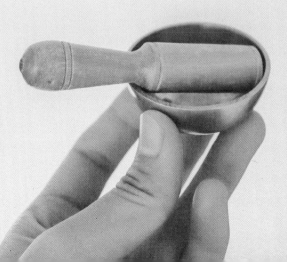

CONTENTS

MY JOURNEY

For a total of seven years I lived in the hectic and fast-paced environment of New York City, hoping for a glamorous life full of luxuries. I idolized the abundance of jobs, the potential for success, and the overall prosperity. City life drew me in with all the skyscrapers, well-dressed attractive people, gourmet food, and the gathering of intellectuals and celebrities. I hoped that I could also obtain the status and wealth that I saw around me. Living in the city was the promise of having more, doing more, and being more. I thought it was a pathway to obtaining a higher state of satisfaction and contentment, and an overall boost in self-worth, all through material gain.

In the beginning, I imagined myself in New York juggling everything with perfection, both professionally and in my personal life, while enjoying the privileges of abundance and overflowing resources. I believed that I'd be living the dream life like all the other people I saw. But it turned out that the "dream life" I observed was only on the surface. Once I realized that reality was vastly different from what I imagined, I understood the real sacrifices I had to make to reach the position I ultimately desired. Everything came with hard work and the readiness to sacrifice precious energy for success.

For the first couple of years my city life was composed of stress-filled commutes, work, school, and personal responsibilities to fulfill. I was on a complete adrenaline rush in a frantic lifestyle. Life for me was about living at a hurried pace and getting as much done as possible. I had no proper rest in between, no time to plan a wholesome meal, hydrate properly, care for my health, and check in with myself on how I felt physically and emotionally. As more time passed, I had fewer opportunities to rest within a highly demanding schedule.

I was blindly running, held captive by my programming of striving and achieving at whatever cost. The only time I felt relief from pressure was when I indulged in consumption as a means of escape and distraction. One of my favorite coping mechanisms was dependence on processed food. I regularly stuffed myself unnecessarily, binging on sugary pastries, including doughnuts, cupcakes, sweet beverages, and loads of caffeine. My other addictions were media consumption, excessive visual entertainment, and impulsive shopping for clothes, beauty products, and fashion goods.

Most damaging of all was my insatiable craving for shopping. I spent my days glued to the computer, browsing online commerce sites, and going on daily shopping sprees. As time passed,

I ended up possessing more than forty pairs of shoes and an unmanageable amount of clothes that were dominating my living space. Every inch of space and storage was covered with clothes and fashion goods. I had mountains of unworn and completely new purchases scattered around, slowly suffocating me and depriving me of any breathing room. I shopped until I was financially broke, unable to pay for a night out with friends.

I couldn't enjoy life or even a peaceful weekend with all the clutter and mess around and within me. I filled my life to the point of wasting hours doing the laundry all day long, spending the whole afternoon attempting to organize some parts of my closet, and spending three hours picking outfits for the week. It was always a hassle to look for what I needed, and I felt more stressed and annoyed by the self-created mess and disorderly space. There was no room to cook, enjoy a long hot bath in peace, or lie down comfortably. Every corner I turned, there was an obstacle, an eyesore, and a contributor to further stress.

As my compulsive behavior worsened and more accumulation gathered, my life slowly deteriorated, heading toward a self-perpetuated downward spiral. Even the mental high and numbness from engaging in mindless activities wore off quickly and eventually led to me feeling more drained. The decisions I had made so far and the direction I was leading myself were taking a significant toll on the state of my

mind, body, and soul. All those years of toxic patterns and unconscious acts of self-sabotage led to complete burnout. I was fatigued, dealing with adrenal problems, sleep-deprived, and suffering with terrible migraines. I could no longer avoid the stress-triggered anxiety attacks and extreme tension of being overwhelmed all the time.

In the end, the signs were there for me to realize that the things filling my life were not sufficient sources of nourishment. I was depleted of the proper nutrients to maintain a healthy and energetic state capable of enjoying life. It had been a long time since I had felt rested and rejuvenated. My mind was always filled with worrisome thoughts about the future and the past. I was on a constant search for solutions to perceived threats and attachment to

seek superficial success. What I needed most was a moment of pause to reset and undo my obsessive thoughts, habitual patterns of repressing my sensations and emotions, and the cycle of physical self-destruction. My body required proper rest, restoration, and time to heal from toxic influences. It was clear that I needed to transform my destructive lifestyle toward a self-sustainable path through healing.

Making the Shift

Once I faced burnout and inner helplessness, I was strongly motivated to counterbalance the damage. Even the most unpleasant emotions and discomfort helped me desire a better lifestyle. Without this realization, I would not have known that I was unconsciously harming myself. It would have taken longer, possibly even a lifetime, to realize that my methods were mindless.

Although it was painful to see my own past mistakes and admit my faults, I had to go through the first step of realizing the purpose of hardship to arrive at a turning point. It was like unlocking a gate that only opened by completing a challenging mission—entering the next phase required strength through obstacles. I felt I could move forward when growth took place within these adversities. Admitting my flaws, undesirable tendencies, and downfalls was liberating.

Seeing how toxic my life was served as a wake-up call to live consciously, no longer blinded by the limitations of the material mind. All the physical and emotional distress pointed in the same direction, telling me to awaken from mindlessness and forgetfulness and finally open my eyes to invite awareness. I realized that life had handed me a harsh but much needed lesson.

Going through a tough phase was the most effective way to get motivated onto the path of self-improvement. I was put on a new journey to upgrade the tools I'd been using to navigate life. What was old and outdated needed to be replaced by more effective paths to long-term benefits. It was a moment of rebirth, a fresh start to create something new, more desirable, and, most important, more compatible to my unique needs. I had all that I required to make the shift through positive lifestyle changes.

The Beginning of Minimalism

Minimalism manifested on my path in the form of the popular book titled *The Life-Changing Magic of Tidying Up* by Marie Kondo, a Japanese organizing consultant and author. Her methods focused on keeping only what sparked joy. My sister recommended the book soon after I had decided to walk the path of healing and life improvement. I was attracted to the idea of letting go of most of the belongings I had, especially the unwanted clothes, as they were a dominant contributor to stress and chaos. They were a major hindrance to the expansion I wanted to invite into my life. More than anything, I needed a deep decluttering and purging of unnecessary things to prepare for the changes to come.

The method outlined in Kondo's book emphasizes awareness of positive emotions and feelings of joy when holding an object. If an item sparked joy, I let myself keep it, and if it didn't, I let it go. With this as my framework, I was able to downsize more than half the possessions in my space. The initial phase took one whole week of deep decluttering. I mainly focused on getting rid of makeup, beauty-related products (unless it was for basic skin care and body care), uncomfortable shoes, and old clothing. I also revisited most of the extra items I kept around "just in case," including stored kitchenware and household items.

This initial step wasn't so difficult, since most of these objects didn't hold much meaning or intimate connection to me. The next round was more challenging. It consisted of weekly decluttering sessions for three months to steadily eliminate any remaining unwanted possessions, including valuables. I began donating or reselling designer clothing, expensive electronics, and items with sentimental value. It was difficult to move forward at first, but later I invited the thought that luxuries and material goods no longer defined my worth. I felt that I deserved better things in general. For items with sentimental value, I reminded myself that the feeling and intention behind the object was more important than its physical representation. It felt easier once I learned to release some of the old attachments about status, physical identity, and material association.

The third round of decluttering came one year later when I moved out of New York to align more with a slow-paced lifestyle. That was when I removed most of my furniture and decided to live an almost furniture-free lifestyle. I only kept functional essentials, basic necessities, hobby goods, and a moderate amount of decor for aesthetic purposes. I replaced the old pieces with lightweight options, including floor cushions, a collapsible table, a hammock, and a floor mattress as a bed. Once I took this big step and committed to making the switch, I felt content with the alternatives. This provided me with the distinct advantage of being able to move and travel easily, free of extra baggage. As a result, my life and personal space felt more expansive, spacious, and full of potential.

I gradually made ample room for more nourishments to enter my life. Without force or striving, I naturally attracted more growth opportunities. I had time and space to invite other supportive practices, including yoga and natural movement. I also invited changes I once feared or hesitated to commit to, including more outdoor adventures, adopting my first cat, hosting guests and friends for sleepovers, and curating my intimate world with selected goods that served as continuous sources of joy.

When downsizing, I made incremental changes to arrive at what I later called extreme minimalism or low-furniture living, and a digital-nomad lifestyle where I could travel freely. I took a slow approach to manifest my desires and needs by releasing the pressure, stress, and perfectionism during the letting-go process. Taking a gentle approach helped me emphasize the precious moments unfolding within the process while safely arriving at the rewards. I was free to take breaks, make adjustments within my space, and envision carefully how I wanted to proceed. From the beginning, I wanted to curate my lifestyle without being forced to change abruptly or adopt a set idea of how minimalism should look. My transition was less about getting it done and living the ultimate simple life than learning through the transition what was most compatible.

Choosing to approach decluttering as an experiment allowed me to surrender most of my hesitation to declutter in the initial stages, even with items that were more challenging to let go of. I decided not to pressure myself unnecessarily to reach the often idolized version of minimalism as complete bareness or emptiness. Instead, I allowed myself to concentrate on figuring out what my preferences and comfort level were. I also wanted to respect my artistic side by having decor, unlike the sanitized version of minimalism. All of this was possible because I emphasized applying what I learned over the past few years through numerous books, videos, courses, and resources in combination with my personal needs.

Within the process of letting go and adopting a minimalist lifestyle, I realized that it was most important to create my version of the practice. It was not enough to follow trends or strictly abide by a set rule, but rather I worked cooperatively with myself. That way, the whole decluttering journey became a source of emotional nurturing and a zone of exploration, not another ego trap of self-comparison or craving. Following blindly only resulted in obsessiveness about seeing results and dependence on the subjective nature of other people's opinions. The key to enjoying the process was aligning with my own self-approval by setting my own standard of what was enough for me.

Once I learned to take it easy, through much trial and error, it felt effortless to maintain a simple lifestyle. It was all possible, even as a recovering shopping addict, because I followed through as much as I could and emphasized making small incremental changes. I took the stress-free path

of being flexible without interrupting other areas of my life. I was focused but not obsessed to the point of neglecting my personal and professional responsibilities. No deadlines were chasing me, and no anxious thoughts rose about doing it perfectly and completing it in a set time. I had all the experimentation and the ups and downs to explore and find what worked for me.

What was most different about my life after starting minimalism was that my inner voice was fully heard and acknowledged. Unlike my past self, who blindly followed trends and was easily persuaded by marketing, I now felt willing to prioritize what I wanted to consume, wear, and fill my life with. It mattered to me greatly how I curated my life to express my freedom to make decisions and my confidence in myself. I learned with the process of letting go that the most valuable lesson was finding out who I was, independent of learned beliefs, external identity, social role, and cultural persuasions. Through deep decluttering I uncovered the power to be myself and influence my surroundings to match who I was within.

Emotional Decluttering

My next step, emotional decluttering, came about when I was brainstorming a way to better cope with feelings that led to attachment. One of the biggest problems I was still facing was passively allowing inner negativities to accumulate without gentle correction or positive reminders. I unconsciously attracted limiting thoughts by gathering unwanted emotions without letting them flow and dissolve by neutralizing the triggers.

While consistently decluttering, I later realized that the safest and easiest way to deal with any burdensome obstacles was to process upheavals in the moment on a day-to-day basis. It was less stressful and overwhelming to handle small amounts of clutter than to attempt to process what was beyond my capacity. Doing it one step at a time at a consistent rhythm was the most intuitive way to approach letting go without the pressure to release so much all at once or to avoid it altogether.

The gentlest way to practice emotional decluttering and minimalism as a complete practice was to notice unwanted forces while they were still new and fresh. This meant taking a moment to pause and be still to sit with my feelings. Detecting the rise of negative emotions as they occurred naturally corrected and prevented negligent patterns of avoidance and dependence on distractions. Becoming fully aware and patiently processing the feelings and sensations was the most effective way to prevent accumulating the worries associated with the emotion.

I learned through many attempts that although it was easy to think that certain emotions didn't matter, taking note of even the most trivial overlooked feelings helped me make significant progress. All the inner work and the practice of letting go, regardless of how small it was, contributed to releasing the hidden determinants of addic-

tive behavior underneath the clutter. It mattered a lot to take notice of the details unfolding in my life and not to miss the precious lessons discovered only in the present moment.

Returning to Sustainability

Adopting sustainability as my next course was seamlessly integrated as a part of my overall practice of minimalism. After establishing a simple lifestyle and safely transitioning into minimalism, I naturally entered into a time when I cared deeply about my consumption habits and their effect on my surroundings. Further study led to learning about how my past habits were detrimental to the well-being of Mother Earth. My mindless consumption pattern and unhealthy diet

had direct consequences that I was unaware of until I became a minimalist. I now knew through self-education that repeated poor decision-making in my life contributed significantly to the clutter and pollution of our environment from the use of chemicals and wasteful resources.

I opened a new chapter in my life about the importance of eco-friendly practices as a part of simple living and a natural lifestyle. I now had the understanding that my actions directly impacted all inhabitants of the Earth, and I was in some sense responsible for cleaning up the mess I created in my past ignorance. Knowing the possible harm I have done led to my strong desire to correct my habits to help the whole of life recover, to purge the natural world of harmful influences, and to heal any human-caused imbalances. I wanted to be available as much as possible to transform my past suffering, and to focus on counterbalancing any negatives.

Realizing that sustainability is an essential practice led me to shift from practicing for self-benefit and caring only for my intimate space to providing selfless service to my environment, a more inclusive and wholesome practice. I thought deeply about ways to better all lives, not just my own. I knew we could all thrive, and not just survive on the extraction of resources and the exploitation of other life forms, as we have done for too long. The next step was figuring out how to adopt a greener lifestyle and to implement my intentions on a consistent basis to promote change. As my first action, I decided to eliminate unnecessary waste, replace single-use disposables, switch to biodegradable materials, and as much as possible be a conscious consumer. The larger goal was to gradually shift toward a low-waste lifestyle, conscious of my contributions to landfills and natural habitats.

As a new practitioner, I began to implement gentle corrections in my everyday habits so I could change without too much pressure. I focused on adopting additional small changes that were easy to implement, including consuming only natural materials instead of those with chemical pollutants, choosing small shops with transparent labeling instead of mega-chains, and focusing on sweatshop-free handmade goods instead of mass-produced factory products. I swapped out my toxic skin care, hair care, cleaners, and detergents, and I eliminated harmful chemicals, artificial fragrances, perfumes, preservatives, and carcinogenic agents commonly used in homes and for personal care. My preference to go natural and earth-friendly allowed me to approach shopping for household essentials as an informed buyer, considering the source, origin, material, and ethical factors of each item I purchased and invited into my life and the home of my family.

Other methods of adopting eco-friendly habits were available when I eased into the practice and felt comfortable with these newly established greener routines. The following year, I made additional efforts by transitioning to a chemical-free and nontoxic lifestyle based on organic living and natural consumption. I took the next step of growing some of my own food at a local community garden and in my apartment to promote organic gardening. I also focused on purchasing organic produce within my budget when grocery shopping. I was open to exploring more self-sufficient methods of living to lessen dependence on farming methods that may be detrimental to the soil, water, and overall quality of the Earth's elements and the present and future lives of other living beings.

The main focus for me in adopting organic gardening and building a more intimate relationship with my food and the natural world was to support a plant-based lifestyle. Since the beginning, I wished to significantly reduce the use of animal products and the consumption of meat during my transition and ultimately to arrive at eating a whole-food plant-based diet. Ever since I planned to change my lifestyle in positive ways, I felt strongly driven to transition from a standard American diet to letting go of all processed food, growth hormones, antibiotics, chemical additives, and ingredients from less compassionate sources.

Leading a plant-based lifestyle for ethical, spiritual, and health reasons felt natural, as I was ready to take larger steps in cleansing my inner world, helping all of the Earth's inhabitants and actively reducing the main contributors of greenhouse gas emissions and climate change. I felt eager to change and once I switched my diet and adopted veganism as a core practice of sustainability, my consumption habits were exclusively based on non-animal-derived ingredients that were free from sources of cruelty, exploitation, discrimination, added toxins, and unnecessary violence.

Additionally, eliminating unnatural and artificial additives and refined foods led to a deep purging of my mind and body from unproductive sources. My meals were entirely based on water-rich food, including an abundance of fruits, leafy greens, vegetables, nuts, seeds, and other plant fuels. This was vastly different from the ingredients that irritated and inflamed my body in the past. Eating what came directly from Mother Earth in its purest form allowed me to feel at my best, which I had not experienced for many years. I saw dramatic improvements, with increased energy, more vitality, mental clarity, and better focus. I also went through numerous positive bodily changes, including my skin clearing of eczema, the end of migraines and brain fog, and naturally correcting constipation, chronic bloating, and digestive issues. On an emotional and mental level, I felt less irritated, anxious, and unable to focus.

In addition, I naturally dissolved my past disorderly eating habits, restoring a balanced and comfortable weight. I no longer suffered from binging, swallowing without chewing, uncontrollable cravings, and overeating. My newly established practice and life-saving knowledge about my personalized nutrition plan from many teach-

ers and professionals led to a healthier relationship with food and a new appreciation for the miracle of plants, Mother Earth, and the body's inherent ability to heal and recover.

Since the beginning, sustainability has always been a lesson on interconnectedness and the importance of coexistence. All the rewards and positive manifestations I saw as an individual through my body were shared equally by all dwellers on this planet. Everything I gave to the Earth came back to me double, and the love I expressed inward always reflected outward to benefit others. My daily commitment to my discipline and eco-friendly practices helped preserve habitats, save the precious lives of other living beings, and restore the Earth's balance, even if it was a small contri-bution. I kept up with my new habits because I strongly felt and recognized the benefits both within me and around me. Every positive inward consumption and outward creation left a significant impact on my own life and the environ-ment as well as the world as a whole. Knowing this resulted in joyful feelings of togetherness and the acceptance of eternal belonging.

Inviting Mindfulness

Connecting the inner world and the outer world allowed me to uncover the next step of making peace within and around me. My next step and focus was on discovering a lifelong practice that provided refuge, a place of quiet serenity within me so I could remain still during passing storms.

The next step for me was to explore mental hygiene techniques to invite stillness even when I faced adversities in my personal life. My deepest desire was to maintain inner peace and calm without stressing over the source of mental irritation or emotional turmoil, which only perpetuated the feeling of disconnection.

During this time, in my calling for peace, I manifested one of the most valuable sources of infinite wisdom I encountered in my journey. I was offered a book titled *The Miracle of Mindfulness* by Thich Nhat Hanh (affectionately called "Thay," which means "teacher" in Vietnamese, by many of his students around the world), a Buddhist monk, peace activist, and the founder of Plum Village, a monastery in southwest France. His mindful words, insights, and peaceful energy deeply resonated with me in my need to cultivate tranquility in uncontrollable areas of life. His presence and gentle guidance served as a turning point in my realization of how important it was to release mental chatter, attachments to thoughts and positions, and the habit of mindlessness as a part of my practice of minimalism and a more complete life change for internal and external healing.

Following Thay's teachings as a new student deepened my established practices of letting go and gave strength to the wholesome values I already held about prioritizing compassion. My learnings began with inviting mindful breathing, daily sitting meditation, mindful eating, deep listening, right speech, and easy-to-do mindfulness-based exercises within everyday activities. For the first time, I worked on correcting my habit of overthinking and a pessimistic attitude by redirecting attention away from useless mental activities. Instead, I focused on walking with awareness, chewing my food thoroughly, washing the dishes with more attentiveness, and living with more persistent focus.

I seamlessly incorporated the teachings Thay generously offered to invite the miraculous healing power of mindfulness within my work, home, and overall lifestyle. I didn't have to disturb what I was already doing; I simply approached my daily life with heightened awareness. This made all the difference as I noticed how much more patient and at ease I was without chasing after mental formations, anticipating the future, planning excessively, craving solutions, or regurgitating past occurrences. My life was dramatically more enhanced just from the touch of mindfulness.

Experiencing the healing benefits of mindfulness led to me attending on-site retreats and mindfulness programs, called Days of Mindfulness, at one of Thay's monasteries in the Plum Village tradition. This was my next big step, to fully experience and temporarily dwell in a nurturing environment where all of life's expression, including eating, working, cleaning, and caring for our daily tasks, were based on mindful intent and deep breathing. The change of surrounding provided a sacred place for all practitioners, the opportunity to be immersed in the slow pace of practicing within the sangha the essential teachings of Thay. Within the retreat, we spent some days going on hikes, walked the nature paths, raked the leaves, tended to the garden, drank tea, participated in Dharma sharing, meditated as a community, and engaged in simple activities.

My actions and outward energies were based on simplicity for the duration I was immersed in the retreat program. Unlike my days before joining the retreat with everyone else practicing mindfulness, engaging in repetitive tasks or activities that seemed mundane had a profound effect, resulting in a powerful cleansing experience from all the rushing, impatience, frustration, and hyperactivity. Living mindfully within a community revealed how precious it was to live peacefully together. My eyes were open to see, my ears were open to hear, and my heart opened to receive and give. It was such a big difference from how I used to feel in my past, blinded by material gain and success.

Returning to another retreat the following year and continuously practicing meditation on my own time and with a local sangha back at home led to the understanding that life became easier not through perfection or eliminating suffering but through being centered even in times of hardship. To me, being mindful was not about arriving at pure bliss or removing all obstacles in life, but rather being in the moment. Even suffering lost its potency when allowed to flow and drift

away as I became detached from it and more focused on the things that actually sparked joy and gave birth to smiles. I only needed to realign and direct mental energy to more nurturing experiences within the present to let the universe take care of everything. I focused on what I loved, and peace became readily available.

Practicing Wellness

Establishing practices and progressing with positive life changes resulted in my discovery of powerful self-care tools. I later decided to call these tools, support systems, and methods of pampering myself "wellness," and I applied them consistently in my daily life. Being a practitioner for several years allowed me to build morning and evening routines to cleanse any unaddressed stress and refresh my mind, body, and soul for a new unfolding at a peaceful rhythm. My approach to counterbalance negativities and replenish sources of life kept me on a steady flow of discipline, productivity, and consistent practice without facing stress, pressure, and burnout.

I established a routine within my daily schedule to dedicate time solely to resting, relaxing, and unwinding without work. Doing so repeatedly rewarded me with better clarity, focus, and motivation when returning to life's callings. I felt the benefits of resetting and starting anew with a fresher outlook and more energy.

My focus was mainly on incorporating self-care at prime times of day—

early in the morning after rising, and before going to bed—because I viewed them as sacred windows in the day.

It was best to reserve these two time slots when I was most emotionally in tune, spiritually open, and mentally clear-headed. My subconscious was easily accessible, undisturbed by external influences. My priority within those times was to invite nourishments that I loved, including drinking detox juices, doing a smoothie routine, practicing yoga, doing skin care, journaling about the day's happenings, and unwinding by reading a book while drinking herbal tea.

Giving love to myself through consistent self-care and doing so flexibly without perfectionism allowed me to maintain a lighthearted, playful, and stress-free routine that prioritized joyful experiences. I allowed myself to skip my usual routines if complete and total rest felt more appealing. I wanted to approach the time I gave love and care to myself without worrying about doing it right or feeling ashamed of lazy days. It never felt forced or overwhelming because I allowed my practice to serve my unique needs in a comfortable and relaxed way.

I felt ease knowing that I can return to myself, my sacred time alone when feeling stressed. I was gently supported through my own humble acceptance that I needed rest and relaxation, like all living beings.

Healing as a Whole

All four practices—minimalism, sustainability, mindfulness, and wellness—came together to complete the inner and outer healing I had desired for many years. I knew I needed to undergo the process of change. It felt long overdue, and I needed to catch up, but I felt assured in knowing that the pace and timing I chose also had unique advantages. Approaching it slowly, dedicating years to educating myself about each practice, and experimenting with specific tools were necessary to establish a lifelong routine. I knew my commitment to change would pay off with bigger rewards as I continued to savor the meaningful gifts already present.

THE PATH OF HEALING

Why We Can Heal Now

So many of us wait for the moment to heal. We may have been waiting for years, or even our entire life. When embarking on a new and unfamiliar path, some may choose to stop or be passive for long periods without taking action. This was my major block in getting started. The main reason behind unwanted delays is our feelings of anxiety about the amount of work and discipline needed to catch up on the lessons we've missed. We focus too much on the intimidating feeling we have when learning about alternative paths and in-depth practices. Mental blocks lie mainly in resisting change or disturbing already established habits and dependencies.

We think from where we are now and fall into comparing our current situation with people who got an early start or who have privileges we believe we lack. The gap between our present self and our desired values is assumed to be too overwhelming to reach, the goals impossible to obtain. When facing this as an internal block, it is primarily the inner critic, the judgmental self, repeatedly interrupting our willpower to facilitate healing. That inner voice gives rise to self-created doubts, worries, and pressure, the very sustenance of the limited ego self, as a mechanism of prevention. Thus it is easy to resist the changes we want out of fear that they are too challenging, or we are not capable, or we are not worthy to receive the light of healing.

The fear we hold onto about jumping into the unknown and doing what we believe we are not capable of doing is a false illusion. We are powerful beings, greater than we are currently settling for, and much is effortlessly on the way, waiting to be claimed, even if we choose not to see the potential within. It is a fictional creation of the mind to believe that healing requires sacrificing what we love or hold dear. In truth, we are never forced to push hard. At any time, we can dissolve the belief that change involves hard work and unwanted sacrifices.

The truth about healing is vastly different from these imagined doubts. Through my eight years of practice so far, I have learned that arriving as a beginner has a distinct advantage—it is even better than knowing what to do. I realized that early experimentation is the key to successful recovery from toxic habits and unwanted forces. It was often necessary to go through the inevitable ups and downs to experience a fruitful practice and for me to ripen as a mature being.

The rewards and gifts are much more gratifying and nourishing when we remain untainted by the inner expectations of an expert's intellectualized mind. Breakthroughs and progress feel significantly more potent for early practitioners. A newbie also has the advantage of remaining fresh and pure in the sacred early stages without experiencing the mental traps that may hinder established practitioners.

Arriving as a new practitioner is a lot like learning to crawl as a baby while those around us praise our efforts regardless of how small they are. Even the most trivial matters feel deserving of positive feedback and celebration. Once we mature, as adults we are expected to function capably. The joy and excitement of being young are absent, and we become immune to the pleasures of witnessing humble steps forward. In some sense, it is easier to become less amused or excited when we are devoid of the simple joys of being childish and innocent. So we should cherish healing with fresh eyes as we set foot on the path of recovery for the first time or return after a prolonged pause.

Learning the mechanism of healing and realizing the role of contrast and diversity within and around us will give us the push we need to partake in healing. The obstacles we may encounter and the inevitable mistakes naturally serve as precious components of mental, emotional, physical, and spiritual maturity. Even the emotions we assume were unwanted and the temporary problems we wanted to turn away from will feel much smaller than we thought. We become fully capable of handling all difficulties with our inherent power.

Once we begin, we discover the gems hidden within what we previously wanted to avoid and repress during our doubtful phase. The temporary upheavals do not have to continue casting a shadow over us, preventing us from basking in the light of healing and absorbing the benefits of positivity. All will become clear and reveal its meaning when we no longer distance ourselves from reaching the solution and the source of clarity.

Embarking on our path as a courageous soul will remind us that ultimately it does not matter how well we live, or the best way to avoid errors in our lifestyle decisions. Beginning will positively change our daily routines and habits, but the surface-level changes are only a meager reward compared to the spiritual lessons along the way. A lot of us will experience transformation on a deeper level. That is why we do not currently have to obsess over the conditions and the rightness or wrongness of our life situation. Once we begin, the physical and nonphysical corrections will naturally take place, replacing unwanted forces. It is useful to remember that our work is not in the doing or the material demonstration of success, but in allowing what is ready to take place by dissolving the obstacles and opening our hearts to life-giving sources. Getting out of the way is more important than making things happen through force and cravings.

It will soon come to light that healing is a lot about training the mind, learning about our feelings, and facilitating self-education within the spiritual realm. While healing, we learn the most effective method of conquering self-limitations, becoming bulletproof to hardships, choosing selectively wiser decisions, and polishing our inner skills directly. We all need this time of training as a step to becoming mindful crafters of meaningful creations. The time to heal is in the now, and our place of belonging is waiting for us to return home from a long and exhausting trip.

Our Role in Healing

When healing, our only work is to give way to what is already taking place internally. We simply have to be guided back to the role of being a cooperative component of healing instead of an unconscious or passive healer. Doing so will help us restore the full healing functions through the active release of hindrances, including artificial stimulation, unhealthy entertainment, and unnatural consumption.

The practice of removing forces against healing is a lot like the daily weeding of unhelpful habits and thought patterns to support full recovery. We can begin by learning to make peace with ourselves, dissolving unfruitful mental formations, and nurturing the flowers of compassion. Our daily commitment to this simple practice creates spaciousness within, which allows healing to cover more extensive ground and reach deeper into previously inaccessible areas.

Why We Need to Pause

Pausing momentarily before entering into deep healing will help us become humble observers of our past. At this time, most of us take a moment to breathe and humbly accept that what seemed to have worked in our home, career, relationship, and personal life is no longer productive and helpful. Instead, our actions, habits, and routines require gentle correction for improvement. After this realization occurs, we can guide healing light toward deliberate places by prioritizing which areas need to change first.

Why Healing Is for Everyone

The good thing about healing for many of us entering with diverse backgrounds is that it never goes against established methods. We can enjoy the luxuries and privileges of personal preferences and still allow ourselves to focus on recovering from unwanted forces. We can continue managing our work, fulfilling family responsibilities, building our business, unfolding our creative passion, and making advancements in modern life. Our healing process doesn't have to interfere with our current lifestyle or threaten the things we cherish.

How to Trust Healing

Healing is a friend, mother, father, partner, sister, and brother who is always willing to help, support, guide, and lead the way to feelings of security, confidence, and empowerment. It never abandons, betrays, disappoints, or neglects our needs and wants. It is not bound to the conditions of the physical realm and is independent of all ego traps.

I've learned that trusting the healing process and embracing the path of recovery is the most powerful tool I have acquired in my search for joy and contentment. Nothing beats having an internal support system ready to soothe and help restore the mind, body, and soul to its fullest potential. I can fall ill, full of suffering, and healing will come to the rescue regardless of what state I am in. It will never determine that I am unsalvageable or hopeless.

Not seeing what healing has to offer and the truth about our built-in support system gives the ego false power through doubt. We can return to the reminder that the only obstacle is within, and that mental resistance creates a lack of availability. Trust that healing is ready to kick in every time we are willing to receive help. It is always here to help us reclaim inner balance and a state of groundedness. Learn to let go and be open, and it will always be our best friend.

Why Focus on Internal Healing

Healing at its first stage is imperceivable to the material eye. It occurs below the surface, in a cellular, vibrational, energetic, and nonphysical realm, where our vision has no use. Any positive action supportive of life that emanates healing energy results in internal improvements before it is physically manifested and detectable by our senses. That is why healing is always present before it materializes as life conditions. Once we realize there are stages to recovery and steps to manifestation, we can find relief in knowing what is asked is already here, without feeling impatient.

Looking and grasping during internal preparation is unnecessary when the materials for building are still being gathered. We can conserve our mental energy and put our sensing abilities to better use by choosing to use them selectively, when we are truly ready to witness the full rewards. We will achieve the desired results when we support the internal healing before the physical evidence of our success. The surest way is not to see ourselves and the state of our body, health, relationship, career, or lifestyle as reflections of where we are in our stage of healing. Trust that the inner work is the key to all that we desire, and the conditions will match our faith in the internal.

How to Let Go of the Results

As we embark on this path of recovery, we will understand and accept that peace, health, and well-being are not conditions we can forcibly create by applying effort. We must accept that healing is not under our control. It follows its own natural pace and requires breathing room and space without us vigilantly watching over its every move. Healing will teach us patience as it reminds us that every time we want to rush, it will not give in to our egotistical desires. Regardless of our selfish demands, it will always choose to follow its rhythm, flow, and nature.

We should not forget that healing is intrinsically free and limitless, so the more we force it, the more we work against it and create resistance. It is counterproductive to repeat the pattern of pursuing and craving the ultimate remedy or prize. Instead, we can focus on the diversity and contrast within our practice to realize that the rewards are not at the destination but in the process itself. Let's trust the process and accept that healing is already taking place by affirming this fact through active reminders, daily affirmations, practices, and cooperative participation.

How to Enjoy Long-term Success

Healing is a daily commitment. There is no magic pill or remedy that will instantly rid us of all our negativities and obstacles. The only method that works is consistently aligning with positive energy through long-term practice. This doesn't mean we need to heal every single day and dedicate our entire life to self-care and personal development. It only means that we need to utilize supportive tools to practice whenever we can, in a regular steady rhythm. Our motto from now on is to do what we can and do it with joy. Do not be discouraged; you will be guided through the whole process!

For those ready and willing, be open to accepting the light of healing.

FOUR ESSENTIAL PRACTICES FOR HEALING

The four essential practices for healing are supportive practices we can invite to assist in our inherent healing process: minimalism, sustainability, wellness, and mindfulness. They are designed to work coherently and interactively with each other.

Why Each Practice Is Important

As dedicated practitioners, we can experience more powerful healing by using the synergetic healing effects of combined practice. Each practice works as an interdependent component promoting growth in the others through the shared goal of harmonizing the mind, body, soul, environment, and lifestyle. Even the smallest progress within one of the practices holds the potential to generate positive results and major breakthroughs in all areas of our lives.

For instance, minimalism and sustainability focuses on the shared objective of letting go of unsustainable and unethical habits to manifest a long-term plan that aims to support our natural state. It works together to elevate awareness of our surroundings and restores intimacy with the internal and external. Wellness and mindfulness also integrate well to release emotional blocks and limited belief systems as well as to promote mental clarity more effectively. Try at least two or three of the four practices, especially when you make a greater commitment to create a holistic healing experience.

Each practice and their roles, aims, and unique benefits are outlined below.

MINIMALISM

Minimalism supports our healing by directing us toward an alternative way of channeling our need for consumption and creativity. In minimalism, the required steps of decluttering, sorting, organizing, nourishing, and maintaining allow us to build consumption habits based on mindful awareness, sustainability, and conscious decision-making.

During the initial steps, we allow ourselves to rethink our past purchases to create a spacious, relaxing, and comfortable environment compatible with our actual needs. In the final stages, we begin to invite abundance of proper nourishments and life-supporting elements to help us recover from our past state of emotional and spiritual deprivation.

We focus on building a long-term habit of simple living that is both sustainable and practical. Overall, it is an effective and life-changing practice for us to learn how to thrive and be joyous with what is already here.

MINDFULNESS

Mindfulness connects us with our inner sacred temple through gentle reminders and daily practice. We learn the way of uniting ourselves with the gift of the present moment. We slowly gather the wisdom on how to flow and be at ease while life unfolds effortlessly before us by adopting mindful intention and practicing active mindfulness throughout the day.

Commitment to our practice will shape us into compassionate beings willing to find contentment in neutrality and inner calm. We learn how to dissolve positionality, violence, and destructive energy for the universal purpose of releasing anger, unlove, fear, and ego attachments. We work on being peaceful practitioners by breathing, sitting through contemplation, entering into meditation, and incorporating other mindfulness-based activities.

SUSTAINABILITY

Sustainability is a practice that nurtures all living beings and spreads healing energy not only to ourselves but to Mother Earth. By including sustainable and eco-friendly practices into our daily routines, we actively work on restoring compassion, loving-kindness, and deep connection among all our brothers and sisters and the natural world. We cultivate the wisdom of using natural and clean resources to help heal us as individuals and as the collective whole of our planet.

The big picture is to foresee the future, predict the path we are heading on now, and mindfully prepare all of us for a thriving and healthy life. It is a practice centered on long-term success through everyday responsible actions and the continuous intention to support life.

WELLNESS

Wellness provides us with a safe and compassionate way to bring self-love back into our lifestyle through self-care. It serves as a tool to help us maintain a positive mental and emotional attitude while we continue to undergo the process of healing. It holds us together in times of inner doubt or stress so that we can stay firm in our commitment to support our mind, body, and soul through healing.

By dedicating our energy and time to wellness, we can yield numerous benefits as it contributes directly to the healing process profoundly and powerfully through destressing and deep relaxation. It works as a continuous support system at all times, even in passing moments of discomfort, life challenges, and temporary negative blocks.

How to Incorporate All Four Practices

Inviting healing and transforming negativity within and around us requires time, incremental changes, and gradual progression. It is sometimes easy for eager individuals to follow a rushed pace and an all-or-nothing approach. This can lead to the tendencies we want to transform and overcome, including stress, unease, burnout, and internal pressure. The easiest way to approach healing and embody all four practices effectively is to inch toward our goals in steady and unhurried steps. It is okay to experiment with what personally feels slow and mindful, as this is subjective. Still, a generally slower pace tends to be ideal for most practitioners.

Why Consistency Matters

Consistent application of each practice, or whichever practices are most compatible, is important to continue on a steady rhythm of internal growth and positive physical manifestations. A committed practitioner with experience may try to meditate or incorporate some of the tools in their daily routine. They may need to build this routine for months or years to feel comfortable. They may also require some days to take breaks or short-term pauses. A newly arriving practitioner is encouraged to follow more realistic goals or what feels most compatible.

It is always encouraged to gradually build consistency and experiment with frequency, timing, and the level of commitment in the early stages. To be clear, being consistent does not mean that we must force ourselves to be committed or perfectly in alignment with our set daily rituals, routines, and practices. We only need to focus on meeting our individual plans as much as possible within our schedule, energy level, and needs. It is okay to invite flexibility and moments of pause with intention and still remain focused, productive, and deliberate in our actions. It is important to try our best within our current capacity, even if we may be unfamiliar, inexperienced, or discouraged by the fearful thoughts that all beginners share.

When to Start

Timing can be important, especially for those with a busy or unpredictable schedule. If we rush into healing without being fully available, we may end up losing track of our practice, or forget the goals we set in the beginning, and fall back to old patterns. It can be discouraging to desire healing and positive changes but not to have enough time or resources. That is why it is important always to make the practice work for our individual needs, and not the other way around.

We can be at ease in knowing that all will unfold in the way that is most suitable. We do not have to begin unless we intuitively feel open, ready, and willing to manifest an improved version of ourselves. Once the signs are there, we can start incorporating some of the tools of the practice in the amount and frequency we feel is most appropriate. If a busy lifestyle still leads us but we want to practice, we can always set easy goals that we can meet within a short period and aim to do more when possible. We can also designate one of the practices as the main focus and invite other supportive practices from the other three options in later stages.

PRACTICE GUIDE

Why a Guide Is Useful

The tools outlined in the following pages are guides for incorporating the four essential practices for healing. These simple exercises include prompts, challenges, and helpful suggestions that serve as methods of self-exploration and self-reflection with focus on fueling positive changes. Each page will help us gather our thoughts, process our emotions, reevaluate our habit energy, and set healthier goals to prepare for the healing that will take place within and around us.

Using a guide or another support system can help us experience clarity, better focus, and awareness within our lifestyle transformation. It allows us to carry out the necessary action and the work for positive change while being able to brainstorm the steps. We will unfold the changes we want to make while being gently guided through our healing experience without the sense of confusion that most face when entering unfamiliar ground. Working within a structured study mechanism or a focused path can help us feel safe, supported, better prepared, and at ease during life changes.

Why It's for All Levels

Practitioners of all levels, including beginners, intermediates, and advanced practitioners returning to their inner work with a fresher outlook, will be guided through practical methods of making lifestyle changes. Designed to be suitable for anyone, this simple guide can easily be utilized without interrupting established routines and schedules. All the exercises in the guide are aimed to be gentle suggestions that the practitioner can freely explore, and none require forced commitment. Once we begin, we will experience the joy of inching closer to our desired manifestation.

Why There's No Deadline

We can take as much time to experiment with what is learned within the guide and choose to selectively incorporate what is most compatible for our unique needs and current capacity in our own time. The exercises in the guide are designed to be supportive and nurturing without a set deadline. We don't have to rush through the process or forcibly change our lifestyle abruptly and end up depriving ourselves of precious opportunities for learning, adjusting, and experimenting. We can dissolve the expectation that we should hurry, excel, perform perfectly, or become 100 percent in alignment with the teachings as soon as possible. If any inner resistance, doubts, confusion, or hesitation arise, feel free to skip it, rest, and take it easy. We are free to allow ourselves to do what we intuitively feel is most appropriate to heal at our own pace through flexibility.

How to Pause Mindfully

As mentioned previously, it is okay to invite breaks, pauses, and lazy days to approach our practice with flexibility. But it is also encouraged to be observant of the intention behind our need to be away from our practice. We do need to challenge ourselves if we want our inner work to be rewarding and fulfilling. We can go about it at our own pace, but we have to remember not to fool our intuitive selves when slacking unnecessarily and making too many compromises. If our goal is to benefit from the life changes we are continuously making, we must incorporate the practice as much as possible. We are our best judge for how much is enough, when it is most appropriate to pause, and timing our return to practice.

How to Include Other Tools

It is encouraged to utilize this guide as the foundation of our practice. If needed, we can invite additional tools, including books, courses, videos, and other resources focused on similar topics or the wider genre of personal development.

Frequently Asked Questions

How to Prepare

Each part of the guide includes a dedicated frequently asked questions (FAQ) section that offers suggested methods to maneuver any challenges or doubts that may naturally arise while implementing the tools outlined. These are basic guides to common obstacles that newly arriving practitioners face and more established practitioners may need reminders on. Feel free to refer to this section for clarification and further insights if the need for realignment rises.

To prepare, it is suggested that you invite a writing tool or digital device to take notes and record answers to some of the questions outlined in the prompts. A journal is most suitable for this purpose, as you can write personal reflections during the process and share your deep emotions. Alternatively, you can choose to simply take mental notes if needed. Optionally, you can designate a sacred space within your dwelling space, removed from distractions, to immerse yourself into the guided healing experience. This can help invite your practice with more focus, comfort, and productive energy without unnecessary elements diverting attention from the precious time of inner work. It is okay to invite calming music, animal companions or any supportive presence, a cup of tea, or a warm blanket.

Other than that, you only need the willingness to be present and to share unconditionally without repressing your authentic beingness. You do not have to hold back in this moment of openness and letting go unless you are doing so purposefully and willingly. We are here as beautiful and humble souls walking side by side as fellow practitioners equally sharing the experience of the diversity of life.

MINIMALISM

What is minimalism?

Minimalism is the practice of releasing what is unwanted by letting go and surrendering the accumulation of negative emotions, mental attachments, and physical distractions.

What is decluttering?

Decluttering is a tool for letting go of unwanted possessions and internal attachments to detox and cleanse our personal space, mind, body, and soul from toxic forces. It involves identifying the unwanted forces, physically removing them or mentally letting go, and maintaining a clutter-free state through observation and awareness.

Why did you become a minimalist?

My attraction to a simplified version of my lifestyle manifested due to negativity I experienced through years of shopping addiction and toxic habits. I was deep in financial debt, unhealthy eating, social media dependence, unwholesome relationships, and overall attachment to destructive consumption. I felt desperate to overcome the mental and emotional challenges I faced due to neglecting myself and my mindless patterns.

Being at my lowest motivated me to seek an alternative way of approaching different lifestyle areas, including my health, diet, finances, career, entertainment, and overall habits. I felt a strong need to let go of the unwanted forces and rise above my inner attachments to feel more grounded, relaxed, and empowered.

How did you start minimalism?

The first step I took to simplify my life was to prioritize decluttering fashion goods. Clothing, shoes, accessories, jewelry, and beauty products were the most significant source of clutter within my personal space. I referred to practical guides in decluttering books and online sources to help me through the process.

What are the benefits?

Minimalism is a practice designed to attract internal and external growth when we feel stuck or unable to move forward. It naturally removes unwanted obstacles through decluttering, letting go, cleansing, purging, detoxing, and overall simplifying life. The most rewarding aspect of the practice is experiencing an improved quality of life by restoring proper flow and balanced energy. All of this allows us to experience the fullest of our emotional depth, senses, mental capacity, and life experience without physical distractions and self-created limits.

What will change by being minimal?

Practicing minimalism releases the burden of maintaining an unsustainable lifestyle. We worry less about having enough money, resources, space, and time because we consciously remove any life-draining forces. We can move freely, travel, and seek healthy adventures without stressing about unwanted baggage, possessions, or limitations. Overall, we feel light-hearted and more easygoing because our lifestyle supports independence, creativity, and freedom.

As we continue our practice, the benefit never ceases as our state of inner freedom and abundance encourage us to maintain a productive, self-driven, and self-motivated approach to life. We are fearless to make additional changes and shifts to further improve our finances, career, relationships, and overall personal development. Sources of energy and inspiration come from all directions as we expand and continue filling our lives with joy, pleasure, and wholesome entertainment. Most of what sparks happiness is simple, healthy, rewarding, empowering, and most importantly, positive for ourselves and others.

Are all minimalists the same?

All practitioners unfold unique practices and hold different approaches within their lifestyle choices. Not all minimalists utilize the same methods or live in a designated way. The joy in adopting a simple lifestyle is mainly filling our lives with what feels most nourishing and compatible with our individual needs, free from external influences. There are no set rules to how a minimalist should behave, live, or consume.

A minimalist as a preference may choose to apply their practice in areas of their home or surrounding space. Some also choose simple styles for their personal fashion and belongings. But a practitioner is not necessarily limited to adopting simple living for aesthetic purposes only. They may expand into simplifying their routine, finances, work, relationships, and overall lifestyle.

Minimalists generally experience a higher quality of life with greater availability of time, space, resources, and more freedom overall. They tend to focus more on nonmaterial experiences, including traveling, wholesome entertainment, healthy relationships, and bonding over physical rewards and material consumption.

Who is minimalism most compatible with?

Minimalism is available for all those desiring a simplified version of their lives. It is not limited to those who currently have more decision-making power or resources. Practitioners in family settings, people with roommates, and both young and old all practice alongside us by choosing to cater to their personal needs. We are all free to create our version of simple living, set our own rules and standards, and approach decluttering within our capacity without limits to our experience level, background, and life circumstances. We will all unfold diverse paths, experience growth, and reach answers.

Do minimalists own as little as possible?

Minimalism is unique to each practitioner, so we are not required to follow a designated number of things to own. We are free to choose what to let go of and keep depending on our lifestyle, preferences, and belief system. The only guideline is always to focus on moderation, balance, and humbleness. It is necessary to observe why we want to hold onto certain things and ask if it is out of unhealthy attachment or out of true need. We only have to be honest with ourselves in our decisions about what is wanted and unwanted.

If we feel hesitant about our choices, we can feel free to experiment with different amounts of possessions to see what is most compatible for us. We may want to be more generous initially and later in our practice be open to owning only necessities, even just as an experiment.

Do we have to call ourselves minimalists?

Adopting a minimal lifestyle does not mean we have to identify as minimalists. It is always a personal preference to use labels for the sake of convenience and inclusiveness within like-minded community members. Labels and names may feel superficial and unnecessary for some, which is also understandable and completely respected. It is more important that we hold wholesome intentions within and feel lovingly supportive of our needs and the pursuit of others.

What are the steps of minimalism?

Minimalism is divided into four steps, including the initial work of planning and setting our intentions, followed by decluttering, inviting nourishments, and the final stage of maintaining our lifestyle.

Below is a basic outline of the steps.

PLANNING AND SETTING OUR INTENTIONS

We first plan our goals, create a general outline, and set our intentions before diving into the action part of minimalism. This step allows us to explore our options and brainstorm our own approach before diving in.

DECLUTTERING AND DOWNSIZING

We declutter our possessions by aiming to downsize and create a spacious and comfortable environment. We first gather all our belongings and decide what to keep and let go of based on mindfulness techniques.

INVITING NOURISHMENTS

We invite healthy nourishment and wholesome entertainment to our practice. We begin attracting and manifesting an abundance of experiences and nonmaterial rewards that bring joy and happiness.

MAINTAINING

We maintain a state of moderation and balance by regularly cleaning, organizing, and tidying up. We work on creating a cleaning schedule that is flexible and compatible with our lifestyle needs. We also work on establishing rules for mindful consumption and shopping for basic necessities.

Can minimalists shop?

We are free to do what we want in our individual choices. We can allow ourselves to invite select goods for aesthetic purposes, hobbies, gift-giving, work, and other mindful reasons if we feel them necessary. The only important reminder is to focus on moderation and mindful consumption when it comes to shopping. It is recommended to invite time for contemplation and reflection when cravings or wanting rises within. Feel free to take time to observe whether the intention to purchase or consume something is really wholesome and healthy.

What are the obstacles and challenges?

The temporary challenges of the practice are here to serve us. We don't necessarily have to be threatened by it. We can choose to be aware of it and prepare mindfully without being overly resistant or cautious. The best thing to do is to stay informed and allow whatever arises to come to the surface so it can run its course.

We can be prepared for some common blocks and obstacles, including potential burnout through overcommitment, not being able to let go, competition between practitioners, fear of missing out on life, converting others to the same path, conflict between family members and roommates, rejection from nonpractitioners, loss of motivation midway, external temptation, guilt, and shame when falling into old patterns, and feeling stuck without progress.

The suggested approaches to dissolving each block are provided below.

Burnout and overcommitment. Start small and build the practice gradually in a step-by-step approach. Try planning and laying out how to distribute time and energy before jumping in abruptly.

Resistance to letting go. sentimental items, gifts, family heirlooms. Apply mindful observation of any emotions and thoughts preventing the process of letting go. Invite contemplation and deep reflection to get to the root of why inner attachments are present. Reflect on what the item symbolizes in terms of memory, identity, or belief system. If this method does not work at the moment, revisit the object toward the end of the decluttering process to think it over. Also, entertain ways to substitute for the object by inviting a different kind of nourishment that is nonmaterial.

Competition and jealousy. Focus on individual effort and practice without falling into self-comparison. Return to humbleness when the temptation to feel superior or inferior rises.

Fear of missing out. Direct attention toward nourishments and healthy entertainment that bring joy and happiness. Focus on those good things instead of looking for what makes others happy. In other words, if the need to be distracted rises, find distraction in good things and not destructive methods.

Converting others. Conserve valuable energy for personal work instead of converting, manipulating, or persuading others onto the path of minimalism. Provide informative materials and helpful recommendations if the genuine need to help others arises. Share any helpful lists of documentaries, films, books, research, videos, audio files, and educational courses.

Family and roommates. Be honest and speak to the other party without being pushy. Clearly express needs and work on setting boundaries that accommodate everyone involved. Don't expect 100 percent synchronicity, and be willing to make slight compromises for each other. Explore ways to practice nonviolent communication, mindful speech, and deep listening.

Rejection and judgement. Let the practice speak for itself and focus on walking the talk. Align with empowerment by believing in the power of the practice and not the words or ways of others. Further dissolve toxic judgment through self-care and wellness-oriented practices.

Loss of motivation. Allow fluctuation in energy and motivation to be a natural process. Take time to return to the practice. Invite inspirational books, videos, or talks if needed.

External temptation. Defuse the temptation by seeking alternative ways to fulfill the need. Focus on nonmaterial nourishments and wholesome ways to spend time and energy. Look for ways to engage in healthy stimulation, including physical activities, outdoor adventures, and natural movement.

Falling into old patterns. Think about what changes have been happening that triggered old patterns. See if toxic consumptions are a way of compensating for something else. Focus energy on resolving the root problem itself. Feel free to refer to the "Wellness" chapter for this purpose.

When is a good time to declutter?

A good time to declutter is when we feel energetic, inspired, and motivated. We should have time and energy to commit to something meaningful and life-changing. We can prepare ourselves by clearing out a specific time or mindfully planning around our work and personal schedule.

If we have roommates, we should first speak to the other party and reach an agreement regarding boundaries. Once clear communication and proper boundaries have been established, we can begin to declutter in a respectful and nondisruptive way.

Where do beginners start?

The workbook guides us through various tools to plan, organize our thoughts, explore our goals, and declutter through a step-by-step process. To start, we can first set our intention for our practice by stating why we want to declutter and let go, and why this is important and meaningful to us. Then we can begin working through the prompts and provided materials and start the decluttering and downsizing process.

Is it okay to own luxury items?

Minimalism is not about deprivation, scarcity, and lack. Simple living allows us to invite an abundance of nourishments that are compatible and necessary to our lives. If we decide that we need certain luxury items to be joyous and happy, it is okay to allow them into our personal space. As stated previously, it is only required of us to bring moderation and balance to the number of things we choose to own. If we have a broader budget than most, then that is entirely okay. We just have to remember not to be excessive beyond our limit and capacity.

How much is owning enough?

As long as we feel comfortable, safe, and supported with what we own and how much we have, then we can say that we have enough. At this point, we can finalize our decluttering process and work on organizing and placing the items into designated areas that are most convenient to us. We then can practice maintaining that state of having enough through mindful consumption and simple living.

What does a minimalist do for fun?

As practitioners of minimalism, fun will be based on healthy and wholesome nourishments and not toxic entertainment. Our individual approach will be different from person to person, but it should be focused on creativity and nondestructive activities. Some examples include traveling, reading, writing, watching insightful movies, gardening, engaging in sports, spending time with animal companions, creating arts and crafts, and developing creative hobbies.

What's after minimalism?

Minimalism requires continuous maintenance. We may not declutter or get rid of possession on a daily basis, but we still clean, organize, and tidy up our space regularly. For a more whole practice, we can take the next step to practice emotional decluttering. Other than that, we spend our resources on enjoying our lives.

10 MINIMALISM TIPS

① Make It Yours

This practice is yours, and you are your guide, point of reference, and audience. Focus on what you want to do and your needs instead of allowing others to lead you. Put all your attention on yourself. You can seek advice if needed, but prioritize your inner being before exposing yourself to external influences.

② Walk the Talk

Do the actual practice and put in the work to manifest your goals. Let your commitment and discipline speak for themselves when others challenge your methods or inner doubt rises.

③ Respect Others

You don't need to manipulate, convince, or forcibly change others to make them cooperative components of your healing journey. You simply have to lead the way through your intention and actions and allow inspiration and motivation to serve others naturally and authentically. Focus on sharing, educating, and helping others instead of persuading them.

④ Enjoy the Process

Your goals should not rule over you. Be open to learning through the process and getting closer to your goals through gentle and flexible practice. Pay close attention to the rewards unfolding throughout the whole journey. You may learn valuable lessons and wisdom even before you reach your ultimate destination.

⑤ Ease into It

Everyone goes through challenges and tough moments during life-changing times. It's good to ease into the ups and downs and allow it to contribute to your strength and power. You can learn how to be less harsh and critical of yourself when facing temporary obstacles.

⑥ Be Flexible

If you need to make any changes or take a pause, feel free to trust your intuitive self and follow through. You are already on the path of healing and letting go, so release the worry about falling behind or not doing enough. You are not a lazy or unproductive person for being honest and compassionate to yourself.

⑦ Nourish Yourself

Be generous with yourself when it comes to healthy nourishments. These are the nutrients that will energize, motivate, and sustain you in the long run. Don't forget to reward yourself when you reach a milestone or short-term goal by inviting wholesome activities you enjoy afterward.

⑧ Take a Leap

Allow yourself to be fearless when you know you can do more. Be gentle when you need rest but productive when you can. Release the need to use time, energy, and other lack of resources to create excuses, unless it is a real obstacle. Be honest and true to yourself.

⑨ Embrace Change

Let yourself adjust to change by allowing temporary instability to be present. Be open to adapt and ease into the moment without resistance. Change is good, and it will help you grow and expand your capacity.

⑩ Do the Karma Work

You can expect positive rewards to be present when you are willing to put in good intentions. Be sure to think deeply about the consequences of what you are doing and how you approach it. Make any adjustments necessary to align with the core values of compassion, loving-kindness, sustainability, and ethical practices. Be conscious of your decisions and how they affect you and those around you in the present and future.

SET YOUR INTENTION

Take this moment first to set mindful intentions and clarify your needs before your next steps. This may be your first time paying full attention to your true needs, desires, and wants. So focus on putting aside any external influence, pressure, and persuasions to prioritize yourself no matter how selfish or unrealistic it may seem at the moment. It's okay to give importance to what you want instead of worrying about doing it right and approaching it in the standard way.

- Why do you want to simplify your life?

- What are the most valuable resources in your life?

- What can minimalism teach you and help you learn?

- What are your core values in life?

- How does minimalism support these values?

- Why do you have the intention to live simply?

- Who are you committing to minimalism for?

- How long do you plan to practice minimalism for? Short-term, long-term, permanently, or perhaps you are unsure at the moment.

- What do you want to prioritize in decluttering?

- In which area will letting go have the biggest impact? Living space, relationship, physical health, finances, emotional well-being, mental health, career, and so on.

- How can you inspire yourself if you lose motivation while decluttering or halfway into minimalism?

- What is the most exciting and enjoyable part of decluttering and letting go?

- What is your current pace with minimalism? Are you doing it fast, slow, or other?

- Set your positive affirmation right now. Recite it two times within silence or out loud. Feel free to use the affirmation below. Additionally, you can place a note of your affirmation somewhere visible within your room or dwelling space as a daily reminder.

"I am open to accepting minimalism with gentleness, self-compassion, and deep understanding without forcing myself when I feel discomfort. I intend to be loving to myself through the whole journey, even when I face temporary challenges."

PERSONALIZED MINIMALISM

Minimalism is unique to all of us. We can set ourselves on the path of gentle decluttering and long-term success by first setting our intention and defining our version of simple living. We can approach our practice slowly without rushing to build a firm foundation.

- List five words that you associate with tidiness and spaciousness.

- What is your definition of minimalism?

- Do you think minimalism can be applied to different areas of your life? Not just your personal space but for letting go of mental clutter, emotional blocks, and limited belief systems? If so, in which other areas can minimalism improve your life?

- What are some ways decluttering your space can help you emotionally and mentally?

- How does mental distraction affect a person's life?

- What is a moderate amount of clothes someone can own to feel happy?

- What are some wholesome activities someone can do in life besides shopping?

- Is there something particular that triggers you to go shopping?

- What is a balanced and healthy way to shop?

- What is most important in life?

- What do you want to fill your daily routine with?

SOLUTION-FOCUSED QUESTIONS

The following questions focus on expanding understanding of our thought process and aims to help us find solutions within. Visit these questions to cultivate better focus, clear mindedness, awareness, and better understanding of our tendencies.

- Why did you choose this particular time in your life to let go?

- Who was your biggest motivator? What was your source of inspiration?

- If you committed to minimalism, what would change in your life?

- How will you be able to tell that you've done enough?

- Who besides you would notice the changes?

- Who besides you would be most positively affected by your decluttering?

- What would happen in your life that isn't happening now?

- What are your best hopes? What difference would that make?

- When was the last time you did a deep decluttering?

- When was the last time you consumed something material and regretted it?

- When was the last time you were sure about your buying decision?

- What would be the first small step that you would take?

- What doesn't need to change and should stay as it is?

- What changes have you already implemented to improve your overall lifestyle?

- What have you been holding onto emotionally that might be time to let go?

- In which living area do you want to see the most improvement?

- Could things be worse than they are? How come they aren't?

- What would you like to achieve at the very least?

- What can you do besides decluttering and organizing to feel happy in your life?

- What is one kind word you can say to yourself before you embark on your journey? Choose something compassionate and motivational.

MANIFESTATION PLANNER

We are now ready to brainstorm what we want to attract and create a lifestyle catered to our personal preferences. This is a time for you to inquire about what you enjoy, cherish, and feel drawn to in life. Let's begin laying out the details of your plans and goals.

- Are you willing to make changes to your space to better fit your needs, or are you comfortable where you are?

- What colors would you like your things to be in?

- What materials would you like your things to be made of?

- What interior theme are you interested in?

- What are your recent interests in life?

- What will make your space feel more special?

- How do you intend to make your space comfortable and relaxing?

- How can you create boundaries if you are living with others?

- How can your space support your lifestyle and hobbies?

SIMPLE LIVING VISION BOARD

Creating a collage of our vision can further help specify your goals and desired manifestations. You can focus on visualizing how you want to feel, what your life will look like, what aesthetics you are drawn to, and what emotions your space will evoke. Let's dive into manifestation through powerful imagination through this guided exercise.

STEP 1

Prepare a sheet of paper, board, or a digital device you can make your collage on. Set this aside for now.

STEP 2

Sit in a comfortable place where you feel relaxed and at ease.

STEP 3

Close your eyes and settle in a comfortable sitting or lying position.

STEP 4

Invite the thought of your ideal lifestyle, filled with only the possessions you deeply cherish and love. Think more deeply about the details, including what clothes you own, what space you live in, the kind of interior, the surrounding aesthetic vibe, habits, routines, and how your daily life looks.

STEP 5

Keep imagining and take notice of the feeling present when imagining living the life you want. Continue for at least ten minutes.

STEP 6

When ready, open your eyes to transfer your imagined thoughts onto paper or in a digital presentation. Create a collage of your imagined thoughts. Be sure to include images, colors, quotes, or any visual representation of your ideal lifestyle or simple living.

LESS VERSUS MORE

What do you want to let go of, and what more can you invite by surrendering your attachments? Reflect on what is ready to be released emotionally, materially, and mentally. Then, reflect on what more is needed to serve as sources of nourishments. Examples:

LESS	MORE
toxic friends	time for myself
work hours	awareness of my feelings
old clothing	clothes I feel comfortable in
unused hobby items	time spent with kind people
negative self-talk	self-care practices
anxiety attacks	resources to travel where I want
unused kitchenware	

TABLE OF LIFE

Minimalism brings positive life changes to all areas of our lives and not just our personal space through the availability of more time, space, and resources. Use the questions below to brainstorm how minimalism can develop other areas in life through more abundance.

- On a scale of 1 to 10, how positive is your current personal care?

- How can having more time, space, and resources improve your personal care?

- On a scale of 1 to 10, how positive is your current health and diet?

- How can having more time, space, and resources improve your bodily health and approach to diet?

- On a scale of 1 to 10, how positive is your current fitness and exercise routine?

- How can having more time, space, and resources improve your fitness routine?

- On a scale of 1 to 10, how positive is your current relationship with your family?

- How can having more time, space, and resources positively affect your family members?

- On a scale of 1 to 10, how positive is your current romantic relationship or friendship?

- How can having more time, space, and resources affect your romantic relationship or friendship?

- On a scale of 1 to 10, how positive is your current social life?

- How can having more time, space, and resources improve your social life?

- On a scale of 1 to 10, how positive is your current personal development?

- How can having more time, space, and resources improve your personal development journey?

- On a scale of 1 to 10, how positive is your current self-care routine?

- How can having more time, space, and resources contribute to rest and self-care?

- On a scale of 1 to 10, how positive is your current mental and emotional health?

- How can having more time, space, and resources contribute to your mental and emotional health and overall well-being?

- On a scale of 1 to 10, how positive is your current home environment?

- How can having more time, space, and resources improve your home environment?

DECLUTTERING PATH

We can begin our decluttering and downsizing process once we are fully prepared to move forward emotionally and mentally. Timing is also important, so be mindful of your current busyness in other areas of your life.

If you feel overwhelmed with work and personal responsibilities, you must allow some recovery time to slow down or approach decluttering inch by inch. You don't want your hands full to the point of feeling completely exhausted and drained.

Once you have made the proper adjustments and plans, you can then experiment with the suggested path in the decluttering guide below. Choose which path is most compatible with your current situation and level of comfort.

Consider these options and see if you resonate with any of them. If none of them feels compatible, take time to brainstorm your own method, and write it down or make a mental note of it.

Gentle Transition Path

The gentle transition path is focused on safely guiding you through a step-by-step transition while lessening the chance of potential burnout, exhaustion, perfectionism, pressure, and post-decluttering regrets. It is ideal for those who are easygoing and thrive being patient and grounded.

You'll give yourself the chance to mindfully choose what you are willing to sort through that day without rushing. You'll have the opportunity to pick the easiest things to declutter and let go of, meaning the items you feel less emotionally attached to. This path is most compatible for those looking to practice steadily long-term.

Challenger's Path

The challenger's path is designed for those who want quick relief and noticeable results in the early stages. It is ideal for those who thrive as ambitious and enthusiastic go-getters. You may be more attracted to this path if you want to practice in the short-term or experiment with the practice before committing to adopting it.

You'll kickstart your journey with greater motivation and drive, leading to a sense of accomplishment, fulfillment, and achievement. You'll have the opportunity to tackle the more challenging and significant things, meaning the items you feel more emotionally attached to.

HOW TO DECLUTTER

STEP 1

Recite an Affirmation

Inviting affirmations into our practice allows us to approach our decluttering process with a positive attitude. We can recite reminders that will help us stay motivated and inspired for the good of ourselves and the well-being of all living beings.

   Below are optional affirmations you can explore, depending on the path you have chosen. Sit, stand, or lie down to invite the breath. When ready, inhale and exhale deeply a couple of times. Then invite an affirmation that supports positive intentions and the willingness to do good. You can choose from these options or recite your own:

GENTLE TRANSITION PATH

"I intend to approach my practice with gentleness, ease, and comfort."

"I intend to accept the unhurried flow of letting go and releasing."

"I am a patient and loving person."

"I am willing to manifest freedom at my own pace and capacity."

CHALLENGER'S PATH

"I intend to focus on what matters most to me."

"I intend to manifest the best version of myself through commitment."

"I am a powerful being on the path of manifestation and inner freedom."

"I am willing to do what it takes to be fully supportive of my journey."

STEP 2

Prioritize and Divide

Prioritizing and organizing our thoughts allows us to approach the practice safely and productively. You can take this time to create a simple system to follow for the rest of the decluttering process. In this section, brainstorm which area of the living area or which category takes priority to declutter and downsize.

GENTLE TRANSITION PATH

Which living area do you feel most comfortable decluttering? Which room do you find easiest to organize? List in order what is most important to least important.

CHALLENGER'S PATH

Which living area you feel the most driven to declutter? Which room needs the most attention and immediate resolution? List in order what is most important to least important.

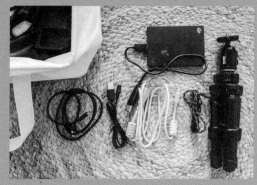

COMPOST

Create a Decluttering List

The next half of prioritizing is dividing the living areas into sections. We can begin by creating a list of things we want to declutter. List them in order of what is most important first.

CLOSET

tops
bottoms
one-pieces
outerwear
sleepwear
leggings
hats
gloves
belts
scarves and ties
socks
underwear
jewelry
athletic clothes
swimwear
shoes
bags
costumes

BEDROOM

sheets
duvets
blankets
pillows and cushions
curtains
furniture pieces
wall and floor decor
other decor
home appliances
small electronics
books, magazines, CDs

KITCHEN

fridge contents
pantry items
utensils

silverware
cookware
kitchen appliances
serving utensils and dishware
baking supplies
cups, mugs, travel cups
bottles
cleaning supplies
dish towels and aprons
storage containers
grocery bags
storage bags
mixing bowls and tools
cutting boards
wall and floor decor

BATHROOM

skin care
hair care
makeup
oral hygiene
soap and body care
perfume
feminine products
medicine
brushes and scrubbers
hair accessories
hair appliances
beauty appliances
shaving implements
towels
rugs

wall decor
other decor
cleaning supplies

GARAGE AND STORAGE

tools and hardware
gardening supplies
light bulbs and batteries
emergency supplies
bike tools
outdoor and camping gear
car tools
yard maintenance
vacation gear
luggage and travel gear
miscellaneous storage boxes
outdoor tools
cleaning supplies
old family mementos and photos
hobby supplies
sporting equipment
holiday supplies

STUDY

books, magazines, CDs
office supplies
stationery
bills and paper records
other decor
hobby supplies

craft supplies
office appliances
small electronics
furniture
wall and floor decor
collections

BABY AND CHILDREN'S ROOMS

books, magazines, CDs
toys
grooming supplies
body care and hair care
other decor
school supplies
stationery
nursing tools
medical supplies
wall and floor decor
games
art supplies
hobby supplies
furniture
sanitary tools
pregnancy supplies

ANIMAL COMPANIONS

grooming supplies
medical supplies
beds and cushions
sanitary tools
toys
furniture

food supplies
pet clothes
carriers and crates
hygiene products

VEHICLES

glove compartment
front seat
back seat
trunk
car accessories
spare parts
floor mats
door pockets
cup holders
visor

DIGITAL DEVICES

social media accounts
email
stored photos and files
browser data
hard-drive files
unused accounts
phone apps
computer files
phone photos and music
subscriptions
notification alerts

Educate and Learn

Now is the moment to invite any learning tools and tips to help prepare yourself before jumping into the actual decluttering in the upcoming steps. Take time to read, watch videos, and draw inspiration from different resources to facilitate self-education.

This will allow you to arrive as a more informed and ready practitioner. Feel free to refer to the recommended resources.

BONUS TIPS

1. Treat your home as a sacred place and not a storage space.

2. Consider that all possessions come with the cost of maintenance.

3. Remember that anyone who lives with you also deserves a comfortable and safe home.

4. Ask yourself what purpose each item serves. Does it meet your basic needs? Is it a necessity for survival? Is it your personal favorite? Does it bring pleasure or joy?

5. Remember that feelings are more important when keeping physical gifts and items with sentimental value.

6. Try to replace an item instead of adding more.

7. Ask yourself if you have used the item or plan to use it in the past six months.

8. Think about the rewards of selling your items and earning extra money.

9. Ask yourself if you would ever repurchase what you bought.

10. Try removing everything in an enclosed space, placing all the items in a separate room, and then slowly introducing them again, focusing on placing only what you love. Seeing a blank canvas will encourage you to be more selective of what you re-invite.

11. Ask yourself if you really need containers, organizers, and dividers or if they are just in the way of simplifying.

12. If you feel unsure and fearful of moving forward, ask a friend or a dear one to help and give honest and compassionate opinions.

13. Remember that your life is precious, and you always deserve beautiful things to fill your life.

14. Think of donating unused items as a charitable act to help others in need.

15. Imagine bringing your dear ones or friends to a tidy, spacious, and beautifully curated space. Hold that thought as one of your goals.

Shift and Sort

The next step is to shift and sort through what takes priority. Focus on going down the list you created and finishing each category and section before moving to the next. Focus on one category at a time, and complete decluttering each section in order.

First, gather all items belonging to one section and individually sort them into six different piles for donation, resale, recycling and discarding, gifting, or storing temporarily. The criteria for each pile are outlined below. Using a box or reusable bin for this purpose is recommended.

DONATE

Things you plan to drop off at a local donation center. You can donate to charitable causes that help the community or support the causes you believe in.

RESELL

Things you plan to resell at a local vintage shop, used goods store, or online resale sites.

RECYCLE AND DISCARD

Things you would instead discard because of its poor condition or any other reason. Follow your local recycling and waste disposal instructions for discarding furniture, electronics, and other specific waste.

GIFT AND GENEROUSLY GIVE

Things you want to give to someone in need. Make sure to respect the receiver's needs by asking directly their opinions and thoughts. Avoid forcing others to deal with your unwanted items.

STORE TEMPORARILY

Things you plan to store temporarily before making a permanent decision. You can put these items out of sight and away from your dwelling space for a short time before revisiting them later. You have to make sure not to abuse this and be mindful of storing only the things you are deeply contemplating. Preferably this pile should remain empty, or be the smallest of all.

Check In

It is important to check in with yourself after your first decluttering session by practicing reflection and relaxation. You have the option to invite deep breathing, meditation, journaling, or any other technique to tap into your inner feelings and physical sensations.

Feel free to follow the journaling prompt below to dive inward. Check in regularly after completing each category, or whenever needed.

1. Prepare a writing tool or a digital device to practice journaling.

2. Choose to sit in a comfortable position free of distractions.

3. Practice a short five- to ten-minute meditation, or simply invite a couple of deep breaths to return to awareness of breath.

4. Once completed, notice any sensations, thoughts, or emotions rising within.

5. Reflect on the following questions.

Which category or living space did you focus on today?

Which sections did you get to?

How did you feel at the beginning of today's sessions?

What went on in your mind during the decluttering and sorting process?

How do you feel now, after today's decluttering?

Do you feel more light-hearted or relieved? If so, what has changed?

What is the thought or feeling that's no longer there?

What was the most challenging part?

What was the most rewarding part of today?

How does it feel to be one step closer to what you want to manifest?

What is one kind thing you can say to yourself for your progress?

Do you feel grateful for anything?

STEP 7

Reward and Nourish

Once you complete the decluttering session of the day, you can take this moment to reward yourself. This is the most crucial step in minimalism, where you invite joy and wholesomeness through healthy nourishment and productive entertainment. You can start your practice of self-gratitude and self-love by treating yourself with positive experiences every time you overcome a milestone and get closer to your goals.

Feel free to choose from this list of rewards:

- Treat yourself to a delicious meal.
- Get together with friends.
- Enjoy family time.
- Cuddle with animal companions.
- Host a potluck.
- Invite dear ones to your new space.
- Do your favorite outdoor activity.
- Enjoy a beautiful day in nature.
- Go camping.
- Practice yoga.
- Take a hot bath.
- Watch an entertaining movie.
- Photograph your new space.
- Share your achievements on social media.
- Visit a gallery.
- Attend a retreat.
- Watch an entertaining performance.
- Listen to your favorite music.
- Play a fun game.
- Go for a walk.
- Enjoy a dip in the water.
- Practice your favorite sport.
- Attend a class you find interesting.
- Dance or sing.
- Be lazy and just relax.
- Do gardening.
- Get crafty.
- Read a book.
- Journal.
- Make art.
- Do skin care or hair care.
- Take a refreshing nap.
- Go biking.
- Try aromatherapy.
- Wear something you like.
- Go foraging.
- Enjoy your favorite drink.
- Sit at a café.
- Visit a park.
- Care for your houseplants.

Maintain

The final step comes after you complete the entire decluttering process and feel content and fully satisfied. When you are ready, you can enter the maintenance phase, building cleaning routines and organization habits. This will empower you in your permanent success of sustaining a simple clutter-free living space.

On a scale of 1 to 10, how important is maintaining a tidy home?

What are words you associate with cleanliness?

What's your level of tolerance in terms of cleanliness?

Do you enjoy organizing things and keeping things in order?

Do you prefer cleaning all at once or doing it bit by bit to maintain tidiness?

Where in the house is the most important place to keep organized?

If you were to pick one, what is the most enjoyable part of maintaining order within your space?

How frequently do you want to clean? Daily, weekly, monthly, or other?

Where is one place that is low-maintenance and least important to be free of clutter?

What can you do to make your cleaning routine more entertaining?

When is the best time of day to clean?

Who will be proudest of seeing your clutter-free space?

Is there anyone who can help you organize?

POST-DECLUTTERING REVIEW

You can reflect on your overall process by sharing your thoughts, feelings, and sensations to bring closure to the minimalism portion of the healing guide.

- Out of a scale of 1 to 10, how much did you enjoy the process of learning and practicing minimalism?

- What was missing in your practice?

- What was the most challenging part?

- How did you overcome that challenge?

- What did you learn afterward?

- Is there anything you would like to improve?

- What was your favorite part of minimalism?

- How satisfied are you with your current space?

- Has it improved in any way? If so, what's the most significant difference?

- Do you feel you have cultivated any positive traits or emotions through this process?

- How did you reward yourself afterward?

- What's your final review about your decluttering process?

- Will you continue practicing minimalism and simple living?

- Would you recommend it to anyone? If so, who?

- What's your next step?

THIRTY-DAY EMOTIONAL DECLUTTERING CHALLENGE

Get an early start on wellness and mindfulness by joining us for the thirty-day emotional decluttering challenge. Together, we can deepen our practice of letting go of what no longer serves us mentally, emotionally, and spiritually.

Pick a challenge to practice each day of the month.

MONDAY	TUESDAY	WEDNESDAY	THURSDAY	FRIDAY	SATURDAY	SUNDAY
Meditate Meditate five minutes to clear mental clutter.	**Be Natural** Accept your thoughts and feelings without rejecting them.	**Be Alone** Focus on your needs instead of satisfying others.	**Reconnect** Write an honest letter to your child self.	**Good Vibes** Be with those who love and respect you.	**Learn** Watch, read, or listen to positive messages and words.	**Create** Express your passion by creating something.
Self-Love Make a list of things you like about yourself.	**Forgive** Empathize with someone different from you.	**Gratitude** Note all the things you appreciate.	**Ask** Ask for help without feeling guilty.	**Say No** Say no to something you don't want.	**Breathe** Take a deep and mindful breath.	**Unfollow** Unfollow negative messages on social media.
Share Share your feelings with someone kind.	**Journal** Journal about something good that happened.	**Compliment** Say something nice to yourself.	**Positivity** Let go of any complaints for the whole day.	**Empower** Make a list of positive traits within you.	**Affirmation** Recite a positive affirmation.	**Inspired** Read an inspirational quote.
Find Joy Do something that makes you happy.	**Rest** Be calm and take it easy.	**Listen** Play relaxing music.	**Smile** Spread your smile to everyone.	**Adventure** Try something new and exciting.	**Laugh** Do something that will make you laugh.	**Remind** Set an alarm to remember something positive.

SUSTAINABILITY

What is environmental sustainability?

Environmental sustainability is a commitment to focus on preserving and maintaining natural resources and the whole of Mother Earth. The purpose is to ensure the health and well-being of all living beings and secure future generations' safety by correcting the depleted state of the natural world. It aims to restore the Earth's pristine condition by establishing eco-friendly practices that help heal and stabilize our planet. Some large-scale projects that focus on sustainability include green technology, renewable energy, green buildings, eco-villages, sustainable agriculture, and permaculture. On a personal scale, individuals can make everyday lifestyle choices by adopting plastic-free, zero-waste, low-waste, composting, chemical-free, or plant-based living.

Why is being sustainable important?

Being sustainable means protecting our only home. All that we cherish and hold dear depends on the abundance of Mother Earth and her unconditional generosity. It is important to take mindful care of our space to enjoy life on our precious planet. Not taking action or contributing to green causes as much as possible can further harm our natural environment and lead to the suffering of living beings, including ourselves and our dear ones.

What are the benefits of becoming eco-friendly?

Climate action, reducing waste, eliminating toxins, and lessening the use of chemical pollutants all lead to the restoration of our planet and the well-being of its inhabitants. We receive improvements indirectly by taking mindful care of our home and actively cleansing the precious resources we depend on for survival, including water, air, and soil. As a collective, we heal and purify everything we consume and are exposed to, further dissolving illnesses aggravated or caused by contaminants and industrial waste.

Internally we also benefit on an emotional and spiritual level through the conscious service we offer. We dissolve the fearful emotions and anxious feelings from thoughts of uncertainty and scarcity through proper planning, preparations, and building of long-term solutions to stressful environmental problems. Negativity and worries are replaced with empathy, understanding, and willingness to implement positive changes for the well-being of all.

How does a toxic lifestyle affect the Earth?

Mindless habits and our unwillingness to stop and observe our intentions and methods can deprive the Earth of its natural resources. Our actions can pollute the air, water, and soil—where we draw energy and food from—resulting in sickness and imbalances within and around us. It can further poison our bodies and disturb the mind and soul. We will continue to face greater inevitable consequences if we forget to live mindfully and consciously as compassionate and caring beings. We will permanently lose the wonder of life, the beauty of nature, precious habitats, fellow Earth dwellers, and all the Earth's miracles if we choose not to awaken from human greed, selfishness, material mindedness, and toxic patterns.

How did you adopt a sustainable lifestyle?

I transitioned into a sustainable lifestyle by incorporating eco-friendly practices within my consumption habits. I began by reducing the use of single-use products, nonbiodegradable packaging material, and items made of plastic. My intention was to focus on what was possible within my capacity instead of aiming to be 100 percent zero-waste or plastic-free. Once I gradually transitioned and introduced low-waste substitutes made of natural materials, including bamboo, organic cotton, and biodegradable ingredients, I no longer depended on single-use products. In addition, I stopped purchasing chemical products and actively avoided toxic ingredients in household products and beauty and personal care items. I also chose cycling as my primary mode of transportation, switched to an electric vehicle for our shared family car, started gardening, and made the life-changing decision to become a whole-food plant-based vegan.

Why did you choose to be sustainable?

Sustainability unfolded on my path as an important part of my lifestyle transformation because I felt a strong need to take minimalism a step farther. I was motivated to heal all those around me as a collective whole and allow my practice to serve a greater purpose. Once I decluttered my personal space, I invited bigger goals and more meaningful projects to let go of environmental toxins, accumulated waste, and pollutants around me. I realized the importance of harmonizing with the world and my surroundings, not just my direct intimate space.

How do we live without harming others?

We can reduce our contribution to suffering and harm by living a lifestyle based on nonviolence. This means actively freeing all life forms from cruelty, destruction, discrimination, forced confinement, violence, and all acts that devalue life. Making an effort to dissolve violence does not mean we have to eliminate those with the power to do violence. It is not necessary to promote healing through destruction or demonization. We can choose to focus on dissolving cruelty and unethical methods by demonstrating mindful paths as alternatives.

Is being plant-based necessary?

We can choose to include the well-being of animals as an important part of our core values. It may feel necessary for some of us to care for the health and happiness of animals to support their sacred lives through loving-kindness. If we choose to take this path, it will benefit all those living on this planet by reducing greenhouse emissions, lessening animal cruelty, and dissolving unethical practices harmful to our shared lands, water supply, and resources. It is recommended to learn more about animal agriculture practices, the marketing of meat and animal products, and the overall effects of factory farming on climate change. Also, feel free to invite proper insights on diet, health, and animal welfare.

What if being sustainable is incompatible with my current lifestyle?

It is possible to face challenges when transitioning to a sustainable lifestyle or adopting new challenges within an already established practice. The best reminder is to focus on what is possible within our capacity. Being sustainable shouldn't be a forced sacrifice. It is good to do as much as we can within our schedule, lifestyle, needs, and resources. We can deepen our practice when we are more available to do so. It is always an option to dissolve pressure or self-comparison by starting small and gradually building our level of commitment.

When is the best time to start?

The best time to practice a more compassionate way of living is always now. There is nothing but the present moment and the life energy filling this time. Our decision to heal together is the most important priority and mission given to humanity. It is recommended that we make some effort to begin as soon as possible.

Of course, we can take small steps to transition and aim higher if we feel comfortable. It is recommended to transition to a low-waste lifestyle with less consumption of plastic. We can then take on more commitment and responsibility by significantly reducing our contribution to the manufacturing of toxic chemical products. If possible, it is also important to adopt a plant-based lifestyle and diet.

We can also explore other highly effective ways to reduce waste and pollution, including composting, natural living, gardening, and more.

What are the different approaches to sustainability?

We can explore different approaches to restoring nurturing energy back into our planet and all living beings through our practice of mindful living.

Some of the practices and movements that focus on sustainable, eco-friendly, and ethical causes are outlined below.

Zero-waste living or low-waste living: A lifestyle based on utilizing all resources to their maximum without creating additional waste. The goal is to prevent trash from being sent to landfills, incinerators, or the ocean.

Plant-based lifestyle: Diet and lifestyle focused on using plant-derived resources without animal-sourced food, ingredients, materials, and products.

Plastic-free living: Lifestyle focused on preventing additional plastic waste by eliminating consumption of plastic materials and packaging.

Vegetable gardening: A garden attached to a house or in a communal setting for growing edible vegetables, herbs, and fruits. Helps prevent commercial waste and supports the ecosystem.

Recycling: The practice of sorting, collecting, and converting waste products into new materials. Conserves resources, reduces energy use, and reduces waste sent to landfills.

Composting: The practice of recycling decomposing organic materials and food waste to improve soil fertility. It helps support landscaping, urban agriculture, and organic farming, and reintroduces beneficial organisms into the Earth.

Renewable resources: The use of clean and replenishable natural energy sources, including hydropower, wind energy, and solar energy, to replace nonrenewable resources such as fossil fuels. Prevents greenhouse gas emissions and promotes diversification of our energy supplies.

Chemical-free and nontoxic living: A lifestyle free of chemicals and toxins found in conventional cleaners, building materials, furnishings, toiletries, cookware, clothing, and household products. It is focused on reducing or eliminating pollutants and poisonous chemicals that negatively impact the health of all living beings and the environment.

Natural living: Lifestyle advocating the use and consumption of unprocessed, organic, and naturally derived products and resources. It promotes nondependence on manufactured and mass-produced products that may negatively impact the environment.

Off-grid living: A lifestyle, architectural movement, and communities designed to promote self-sufficiency without dependence on public utilities. It supports green initiatives, including renewable energy, permaculture, recycling, natural building, homesteading, and composting toilets.

Tiny-house movement: Architectural movement and lifestyle for sustainable development focused on constructing and living in tiny homes to reduce our environmental footprint and resources. Many are built with recycled materials, renewable resources, and earthen materials to promote sustainability.

How can a single person heal the Earth?

As practitioners, we can help maintain a tidy, clean, and safe space for all inhabitants of the Earth, free of harmful chemicals and unnatural human creations, by committing to daily practice as much as we can. Aligning our daily routine and habits to ethical and sustainable approaches allows all inhabitants to feel safe, healthy, and wholesome. In addition, we can focus on the inner work of dissolving selfishness, greed, and most importantly, our disconnection from life-giving sources to restore nondiscrimination and equality. Our personal decisions and everyday commitment to a sustainable path can directly transform universal suffering and pain. It brings benefit to all, heals us as a whole, and restores hope for humanity.

Are sustainable practitioners better than unsustainable people?

The purpose of practice is to focus on our individual contributions and never on competition or separation from one another. Our practice comes from the root of kindness and willingness to offer help for others. It should not derive power, superiority, or righteousness over others or their methods. Let's focus on doing good and spreading love to harmonize and coexist with all living beings instead of creating hostility and separation. We do not have to demean others or think of them as inferior just because we got a head start. All of us will eventually meet and diverge on the same path to work together toward a more sustainable way of existence.

Do we have to be perfect and 100 percent sustainable?

No—like minimalism and other practices, sustainability is also subjective and unique to all individuals. It is not necessary to pursue an ideal version or a state of perfection through the force and unrealistic expectations. We only need to try our best to be deliberate, intentional, and committed to making meaningful contributions to help heal Mother Earth and all living beings.

What if the Earth doesn't get better?

It takes time, consistency, and the willpower of many to see global results. These benefits are usually gradual and steady. But we can always witness the benefits of our practice when we experience health and vitality on an individual level. We can observe how our practice of compassionate and mindful living contributes to mental, emotional, and spiritual growth and helps our mind and bodies recover from toxins.

SUSTAINABILITY SELF-EVALUATION

Assessing our current approach to sustainability and eco-friendly living helps us return to honest self-reflection and contemplation. Use the scale to answer each question with a value, then add the numbers to get a total.

3: always
2: often
1: infrequently
0: never

1. Do you use reusable bottles, bags, containers, and straws?

2. Do you choose biodegradable or recyclable materials over inorganic disposables?

3. When you go shopping, do you bring your own shopping bags?

4. When possible, do you refrain from using unnecessary energy at home?

5. Do you actively look for sweatshop-free and ethical brands to buy from?

6. Do you use energy-saving products?

7. Do you eat a plant-based diet or try to mostly eat nonanimal ingredients?

8. Do you refrain from buying animal products?

9. Do you purchase food that is unprocessed, unpackaged, and locally grown?

10. Do you use renewable energy?

11. Do you compost food waste?

12. Do you recycle?

13. Do you watch, read, support, follow, or expose yourself in any way to environmental causes to educate yourself?

14. Do you try to reduce plastic use?

15. Do you fill your vehicle with gasoline?

16. Do you try to reduce air travel?

17. Do you try to use public transportation or walk instead of using your personal vehicle?

18. Do you turn off or unplug unused electronics?

19. Do you take your waste with you when you are on the trail or outdoors?

20. Do you turn off the water tap when it is not being used?

21. Do you try to bring your own containers when you get take-out food?

22. Do you buy environmentally friendly household products—laundry detergent, soap, brushes, and so on?

23. Do you buy chemical-free or nontoxic personal care products?

24. Do you try to buy environmentally friendly products for yourself and your household members, including your animal companions?

25. Do you try to reuse packaging materials or paper products?

26. Do you try to reduce water consumption while taking a shower or bath?

27. If possible, do you try to fix things instead of buying a replacement?

28. If you had the money, would you be willing to donate to environmental causes you trust?

SCORE

70–84: You are already actively sustainable.
46–69: You are making a reasonable effort.
11–45: You're on the right track; more is possible.
0–10: You're new to sustainability.

SUSTAINABLE ACTION PLAN

We can begin solidifying our commitment to sustainable practices by listing which actions we intend to take as a contribution.

- List five books you want to read related to sustainability.

- List five films or documentaries you want to see related to sustainability.

- List three activities or sustainability advocates that inspire you.

- Write three quotes related to sustainability that inspire you.

- List five social media accounts that motivate you.

- List two nonprofit organizations or groups you want to support.

- List any specific sustainable actions and practices you want to commit to.

SHORT-TERM AND LONG-TERM GOALS

Goals are helpful as sources of motivation, passion, and creative drive. We can create short-term and long-term plans to build our framework and shed light on our deeper needs.

- What are three things you can do within a week to get closer to your easiest goal?

- List three things you can do within a month to get closer to the most important goals.

- List three things you can do within a year to get closer to any of your other goals.

- List three things you can do within a year to get closer to any of your other goals.

- How long are you willing to invest in your sustainable practice? Do you have a preferred period or deadline?

LOW-WASTE SWAPS

Feel free to utilize this handy low-waste swap list to transition toward a lifestyle based on conservation and mindful consumption. Focus on making easy switches in the beginning and taking additional steps if possible.

HOME

LED light bulbs

powdered laundry detergent

reusable tissue

reusable dryer balls

KITCHEN

reusable straws

cloth napkins

cloth towels to replace paper towels

reusable grocery bags

reusable produce bags

reusable food wrap

glass food jars

plastic-free or recycled food storage containers

reusable tea bags

TRAVEL

reusable utensils

refillable bottle

refillable mug

reusable food storage containers

reusable travel bags

cloth handkerchief

tote bag

refillable personal care products

biodegradable toothbrush

bar soap and soap container

BATHROOM AND PERSONAL CARE

biodegradable toothbrush

menstrual cup

reusable menstrual pads

washable makeup pads

refillable deodorant

refillable razors

shampoo bar

refillable makeup

biodegradable and refillable floss

bar soap or refillable liquid soap

biodegradable wooden brush

bulk cleaning products or DIY cleaning solutions

refillable cleaning-spray bottle

BABY AND CHILDREN

reusable cloth diapers

reusable wipes

biodegradable or recycled toys

biodegradable wooden brush

refillable body-care products or biodegradable packaging

refillable cleaning spray bottle

ANIMAL COMPANIONS

biodegradable or recycled waste bags

washable potty pads

recycled or biodegradable toys

biodegradable wooden brush

pet bath soap or refillable liquid soap

SUSTAINABLE GROCERY PLANNER

One step we can take to become more sustainable is to do our regular grocery shopping with more awareness. We can begin inviting reusable items to prevent the use of disposables and make mindful shopping choices to practice eco-friendly living. Reflect on the questions below to get started.

- Can you buy locally grown produce? If so, where?

- Can you buy seasonal produce? If so, where?

- Can you buy from local shops, independent sellers, or mom-and-pop stores? If so, what are your options?

- Do you have reusable produce bags and grocery bags?

- What percentage of your usual grocery list is fresh produce?

- What percentage of your usual grocery list is plant-based?

- Can you buy some of your groceries in bulk? If so, where?

- Can you bring your own bottle and refill your detergent, liquid soap, and cleaning supplies? If so, where?

- How often can you buy organic produce?

- How often can you buy ethically sourced and certified sustainable products?

- Do you know how to recycle packaging materials?

- Can you compost food waste?

- What percentage of your usual grocery list expires or goes to waste?

- Do you know how to preserve and store food for the long term?

- Have you tried pickling, curing, drying, fermenting, canning, or freezing, as a preservation method to avoid food waste?

TWELVE WAYS TO AVOID FOOD WASTE

Below are some valuable tips to make food last longer so it does not get wasted. Consistent commitment can help eliminate resources being discarded and wasted.

1. Keep bananas separate from other fruits to extend their shelf life.

2. Wash berries in a diluted vinegar solution before storing them in the fridge.

3. To store herbs like parsley and cilantro,
   place the end of the stems in a jar and fill it with one or two inches of water. Loosely cover the leaves with a reusable bag.

4. Declutter and clean your fridge regularly to eliminate any harmful bacteria.

5. Wash and then wrap lettuce in recycled paper to keep it dry.

6. Store apples and potatoes together to allow naturally occurring ethylene gas from the apples to prevent rotting.

7. Freeze overripe avocados after coating them with a bit of lemon juice.

8. Freeze leftovers, scrap food, vegetables, and fruits you don't intend to eat soon.

9. Keep grapes on the stem to help them last longer.

10. Place asparagus spears upright in a glass jar.

11. Store mushrooms in a paper bag.

12. Keep garlic and onions in a well-ventilated mesh bag or basket.

ELEVEN MINDFUL SHOPPING TIPS

For the necessities and what is essential for life, we can focus on sustainable and mindful consumption. Below are some tips we can follow to make conscious decisions while we are shopping.

① Look for Sustainable Brands

Be open to buying sustainable or ethically sourced goods when they are available and within your budget. A list of standard sustainable certifications:

USDA Organic (or any other reputable organic certification)

ECOCERT

EWG Verified

Non-GMO

Leaping Bunny Cruelty-Free

Certified Vegan

PETA Cruelty-Free and Vegan

Fair Trade USA

GOTS Certified (Global Organic Textile Standard)

Certified B Corporation

FSC (Forest Stewardship Council)

BCI (Better Cotton Initiative)

STANDARD 100 by OEKO-TEX

WRAP (Worldwide Accredited Production)

Bluesign Standard

② Buy Used

Ask yourself if you are willing to choose used products instead of new products. Used clothes, household items, and bags are often available at local used good stores and online shops.

④ Can You Survive Without It?

Tap into your inner self and see if you can survive without something you've been debating buying.

③ Make Positive Purchase Decisions

Make purchase decisions based on a positive mind-set and not guilt, shame, unwanted influences, or external pressure.

⑤ Be Grateful

Send gratitude and appreciation for all the resources and labor invested in creating what you want to purchase.

⑥ Love It or Leave It

Be 100 percent sure that you are satisfied with the design, brand values, aesthetics, material, and overall feel of what you want to purchase. Pay close attention to any doubts, and see if you are willing to follow your intuition.

⑦ Make It Last

Opt for high-quality materials that will last a long time instead of products that are disposable and easily broken. Stay within your budget but still invest early on to prevent repurchasing.

⑧ Buy Local

Check out local shops and craft fairs to support independent sellers, distributors, and artists. Support your community and help them thrive!

⑨ Get Creative

Explore ways to make it yourself instead of buying it. Seek scrap materials at home or recycled found objects for your creative DIY project.

⑩ Know What You Want

Be intentional and conscious about your purchase by knowing what you want before entering a store or shopping online. Try to avoid browsing to prevent unnecessary temptation.

⑪ Breathe and Meditate

If you notice any temptation or hesitation rising within you, invite your practice of meditation and deep breathing. Go back to awareness and tap into your inner needs before making a decision based on an impulse.

HOME DETOX SWAPS

Letting go of harmful and unnatural toxic chemicals can help us detox our lives. Use the list below to explore alternative options that can eventually replace some of the products you currently hold onto.

NATURAL OPTIONS

Explore these natural alternatives to make the switch.

Home

nontoxic powdered laundry detergent

naturally scented organic soy or plant-based candles

nontoxic castile all-purpose cleaner

vinegar and baking soda solution as a cleaner

unscented toilet paper

cloth kitchen towel

nontoxic castile dish soap

coconut, castile, or other plant-based hand soap

wooden, ceramic, or stainless-steel utensils

wooden, ceramic, or stainless-steel dishware

ceramic or glass cups

glass, ceramic, or cast-iron nontoxic cookware

air purifying plants: snake plant, rubber plant, peace lily, fiddle leaf fig

BPA-free water filtration system

Beauty and Personal Care

coconut oil or natural makeup remover

plant-based and natural paraben-free skin care, body care, and makeup

nontoxic fluoride-free toothpaste and mouthwash

octinoxate- and oxybenzone-free sunscreen

aluminum-free deodorant

Pet Care

nontoxic wooden, paper, or BPA-free toys

ceramic, wooden, glass, or stainless-steel bowls

certified organic or chemical dye–free bedding

Baby Care

linen, hemp, organic cotton, or organic bamboo clothing

certified organic or chemical dye–free bedding and towels

BPA-free utensils and dishware

plastic-free or BPA-free toys

fragrance-free cloth wipes

TOXIC INGREDIENTS AND MATERIALS

Below are chemicals that are considered harmful and may negatively affect the body. Check the label to see if any of these ingredients were used in the product.

aluminum: in cosmetics, over-the-counter drugs, cookware, deodorant

BPA and BPS: found in plastic

PTFE: nonstick pan coating

lead: paint, ceramics, cosmetics

pesticides: conventional food and fabrics

PBDEs and PBBs: flame-retardant chemical found in furniture, mattresses, curtains

chemical dyes

paraffin: candles, wax paper, cosmetics, polishing agents

perfumes and artificial fragrances: cosmetics, personal hygiene products

formaldehyde: fabric softeners, dishwashing liquid, cosmetics, industrial resin

parabens: syrups, beverages, jams, baked goods,

skin care, deodorant, shaving gel, toothpaste, sunscreen

phthalates: hairspray, deodorant, perfume

sulfates: household cleaners, personal hygiene products, detergent

synthetic colors

triclosan: disinfectants, toothpaste, personal hygiene products, soap, detergent, plastic kitchenware, cosmetics

toluene: glue, ink, stain remover, paint brush cleaner, paint thinner, nail polish

talc: insecticides, paint, lubricants, grain polisher, rice, corn

alcohol

PVC: vinyl

bromine: swimming pools, medications, upholstery, plastic products

propylene glycol: bread, dairy products, soft drinks, cake mixes, packaged food

food dyes and coloring

artificial flavorings

BHT and BHA: chewing gum, processed food, animal feed, petroleum products, cosmetics

ethoxyquin: animal feed, pet food

synthetic preservatives

chlorine bleach

DEET: insect repellent

sodium laureth sulfate: personal hygiene products, liquid soap, laundry detergent

HEALTHY DIET PLANNER

What we eat has a big impact not only on our mind and body but also other living beings and Mother Earth. We can take steps to understand our eating habits and consumption patterns to make eco-friendly conscious choices about our food sources.

- What is your current diet? What kind of food does it consist of?

- What are some foods that you consider to be healthy?

- Are you eating enough of this?

- What are some foods that you consider to be unhealthy?

- Are you consciously limiting the consumption of this?

- What is your current ratio of eating healthy and unhealthy ingredients?

- Do you believe your diet has a significant impact on your health and also the environment?

- Do you know of any healthy diets that are supportive of your body and also environmentally friendly?

- Who can you consult professionally regarding your current consumption pattern and state of health?

- Are you willing to eat more organic ingredients, seasonal fruits and vegetables, plant-based food sources, and locally sourced products?

- What can you do to educate yourself about healthy eating and eco-friendly food sources?

- List your next steps for lifestyle improvements in your food consumption and eating habits.

LOVING KINDNESS FOR LIVING BEINGS

Take a moment to reflect on how your actions and lifestyle choices impact other living beings on this planet. See if any gentle corrections or alternative methods can better align with the welfare of animals, insects, plants, and protecting the environment.

- List three things you already do that may benefit the Earth and its inhabitants.

- Take time to read any informative resource to list the top-five leading causes of greenhouse gas emissions.

- What are two ways you can help decrease global warming?

- Are there any living beings you would like to help with your commitment?

- List any additional changes you can make to help support life on Earth, including animals, insects, and the overall well-being of Mother Earth.

- What is one easy step you can take starting this week?

- What is one long-term goal you have?

SEVEN-POINT SUSTAINABLE DIET PLAN

Consider these seven sustainable diet and lifestyle criteria to help plan for eco-friendly consumption habits.

1. Affordability and Accessibility

Ask yourself if you can afford the ingredients and have access to food sources. Do you have time to purchase and prepare food for yourself in your schedule and on your budget?

2. Nutritional Balance

Be sure to consume a nutritionally balanced diet by consulting with a professional nutritionist, dietician, physician, or health and diet specialist.

3. Scientific and Evidence-Based

Read educational and insightful information from trustworthy sources to learn more.

4. Ethical Values

Consider how your choice impacts animal welfare, the environment, biodiversity, waste management, climate change, energy use, water use, and land use. Also keep in mind the working conditions and ethical practices of the places you purchase food.

5. Joy and Pleasure

Focus on doing what you find wholesome and pleasurable. Don't forget to consider your preferences when it comes to taste, your belief system, and your mind-set.

6. Safety and Quality

Think about the quality and safety of your food. If possible, choose fresh organic ingredients, from trustworthy local sources, that will not be detrimental to your health and the well-being of living beings, including Mother Earth.

7. Consider Plant-Based Options

Below are five low-meat or plant-based diet and lifestyle options you can explore and learn about with your physician or health and diet specialist. Dive deeper if you feel it is necessary for your next step in sustainable action. Keep in mind that individual choices may vary, as not everyone follows the same approach; you may need to make adjustments or take a personalized approach.

DIET & LIFESTYLE	WHAT IT IS	REMOVES	INCLUDES
pescatarian	A pescatarian diet and lifestyle excludes consumption of meat and poultry for ethical, health, and personal reasons.	meat and poultry	dairy, eggs, fish, seafood, grains, fruits, vegetables, legumes, nuts, seeds, gluten, oil, sweeteners and cane sugar, processed and refined ingredients
vegetarian	A vegetarian diet and lifestyle excludes consumption of meat, poultry, and fish for ethical, health, and personal reasons.	meat, poultry, fish and other seafood	dairy, eggs, grains, fruits, vegetables, legumes, nuts, seeds, gluten, oil, sweeteners and cane sugar, processed and refined ingredients
vegan	A vegan diet and lifestyle excludes consumption of meat, poultry, fish, and animal-derived products for ethical, health, and personal reasons.	meat, poultry, fish and other seafood, dairy, eggs, and all animal-derived products	grains, fruits, vegetables, legumes, nuts, seeds, gluten, oil, sweeteners and cane sugar, processed and refined ingredients
whole-food plant-based	A whole-food plant-based diet and lifestyle consumes minimally processed natural ingredients in their pure and whole form. Abstains from the use of all animal-derived products for ethical, health, and personal reasons.	meat, poultry, fish and other seafood, dairy, eggs, all animal-derived products, gluten, processed and refined ingredients, artificial ingredients, preservatives, chemical derivatives (MSG), cane sugar, refined oil, refined grains, table salt	whole grains, fruits, vegetables, legumes, nuts, seeds, natural sweeteners, natural salt

COMPASSIONATE ACTION LOG

Spend a whole week committing to compassionate actions based on sustainability, eco-friendly living, and ethical practices. Keep a record of your daily contributions to invite self-gratitude and appreciation.

Pick a week to start and begin spreading loving-kindness. Write down one contribution that supported Mother Earth and one action that helped other humans or living beings.

Letter to Mother Earth

Express gratitude, appreciation, and love toward Mother Earth by taking this moment to share your thoughts and feelings with her. Tell her how much she is cherished and held dear.

In addition, you can direct a second letter to your favorite animal, insect, plant, or living being.

Bonding with the Earth

Pick a day and choose one or two of the activities below to share with Mother Earth. Enjoy a full day of bonding, deeply connecting, and interacting with natural elements.

Tree Hugging

Go outdoors and pick a tree that is in need of healing and love. Bond with Mother Earth through the tree and make friends with it. Tell the tree how you feel about nature and its miracles.

Mindful Walking

Walk slowly and mindfully on a trail or in a park and focus on feeling the Earth through your feet. Take gentle steps without rushing. Send good energy and nutrients to help fertilize and cleanse the soil.

Sending the Energy of Love

Take an element from Mother Earth—a fruit, plant, leaf, branch, or any other resource—and place it in the palm of your hand. Hold it with loving energy and recite a positive affirmation of gratitude.

Feel free to do this at home or outdoors in a natural environment where resources are abundant.

Forest Bathing

Forest bathing (*shinrin-yoku*), a practice originating from Japan, is the therapeutic experience of leisurely walking through a forest. Invite the practice by visiting a trail or natural environment where trees are abundant. Let Mother Earth purify your mind, body, and soul.

Observing the Present Moment

Take time to sit outdoors in stillness to observe the passing of time and changes in nature. Observe how the temperature changes and how the colors and hues change over the course of the day.

GRATITUDE LIST

Create a list of fifteen things to be grateful for in your lifetime. This activity allows us to restore deep appreciation and bond with the resources around us.

1. Close your eyes and invite deep breathing.

2. Recall all the things that continue to support, nurture, and heal you.

3. Use your journal, a sheet of paper, or digital device to create a whole list for you to remember in the future.

4. Come back to the list when you feel the need to remember how grateful you are for the miracle of life.

OBSERVING WHAT'S AROUND

Observing our surroundings with mindful awareness allows us to become more in tune with nature and the elements. It helps us connect with Mother Earth on a deeper level, where we learn how to listen to her voice and needs. Let's take this moment to nurture empathy and understanding, and to be available and open to life around us.

Choose a place to be in stillness: a natural environment or any place you feel connected with. When ready, visit the prompts below.

- Write five things you see.

- Write five sources of the sounds you hear.

- Write five things you smell.

- Write five emotions or sensations you feel at the moment.

- Write five things you observe that are still.

- Write five things you observe that are in motion.

SUSTAINABLE ACTION CHECK-IN

Let's bring closure to what we have learned and implemented through the sustainability portion of the healing guide. You can take this time to check in with yourself, share your feelings and thoughts, and see where you have grown the most. You can also think of ways to further your practice on your continuous journey.

- What changes have you made so far to align with sustainability?

- What's the best decision you made to be more sustainable?

- On a scale of 1 to 10, how satisfied are you with your progress?

- Were you able to reduce the amount of single-use plastic, product packaging, animal-based products, chemical ingredients, or unsustainable and unethical products?

- Did you discover something to enjoy about your new lifestyle—alternative ways to shop, natural substitutes, new restaurants, new foods?

- Did you learn anything new during the process?

- What was the most challenging part?

- Did you inspire, motivate, or spark an interest in sustainability in others during your journey?

- How do you feel now about Mother Earth?

- How does being environmentally friendly make you feel about yourself?

- What emotions and feelings were you able to nurture and deepen through your practice?

- What is your positive message to the world?

- How would you like to reward yourself for finishing the sustainability portion of the guide?

- What's your next step in continuing your practice?

- Are you up for the seven-day low-waste challenge in the next section?

SEVEN-DAY LOW-WASTE CHALLENGE

If you are willing and ready, join us for the seven-day low-waste challenge to promote a conscious and low-impact lifestyle based on reusables, package-free consumption, and plastic-free living. Let's fill our week to create a zero-waste future.

If you are already practicing most of what is covered in the challenge, feel free to come up with new goals you want to invite to challenge yourself.

Monday: Pack a Lunch

Make homemade meals and pack a lunch instead of ordering takeout or delivery.

Tuesday: Go Paperless

Change your mail subscriptions to paperless.

Wednesday: BYOB

Bring your own bag on a grocery trip. Additionally, you can use produce bags instead of single-use bags.

Thursday: Swap for Reusables

Replace disposables with reusables, including zero-waste water bottles, utensils, straws, containers, paper towels, and food wrap. Start using them when you eat out.

Friday: Buy Nothing

Engage in an activity that doesn't require consumption: visit a library, go to a park, take a stroll, or be in nature.

Saturday: Get Creative

Repair something or start a DIY project. Get creative by recycling found objects. You can also make your own laundry detergent, all-purpose cleaner, and reusable rags.

Sunday: Support Communities

Plan a visit to eco-friendly communities and gatherings, including farmers markets, handmade-craft markets, zero-waste stores, bulk stores, community gardens, and nonprofit organizations.

Bonus Day: Go Plant-based

Spend a cruelty-free day without consuming any animal-based food or products. Feel free to extend this process and make it a permanent habit to drastically reduce or eliminate your consumption of animal products.

WELLNESS

What is wellness?

Wellness is the practice of unfolding a higher version of ourselves through consistent application of healthy habits and daily self-care routines. The purpose is to maintain wholesomeness in mind, body, and soul and to promote a thriving lifestyle not limited by stress. It also serves as a holistic preventive measure that reduces susceptibility to illnesses as well as emotional and bodily suffering that may result from poor lifestyle choices. The nature of the practice is in being conscious decision-makers who take responsibility to better ourselves with the resources at hand. A practitioner of wellness prioritizes taking care of their health and well-being to enjoy a satisfying life at their fullest potential.

What are the benefits of practicing wellness?

Wellness provides safety and security when we struggle with emotional upheavals and external triggers. The support systems and healing routines we create as a part of our wellness practice allow us to return to our daily activities with more stability and clarity. It is the best investment we can make to promote long-term emotional and mental health.

How did you start your wellness practice?

I first began my daily commitment to wellness by inviting practical self-care tools that I can easily implement without disturbing my work schedule and personal needs. I wanted to maintain my usual routines to allow self-care to be integrated harmoniously. I decided that it was most suitable to focus only on morning and evening routines, outside the busiest times, to build a doable practice. My first choices were simple skin care, drinking tea, and journaling. Once I got comfortable with the first steps and established a comfortable routine, I gradually invited more nourishments.

Why is self-care important?

Self-care is returning to our inner home and bringing the energy of loving-kindness. Practicing it daily or regularly helps us recover from stress, stimulants, and pressure from work, relationships, finances, and common challenges in life. It restores our capacity for compassion and loving-kindness when we feel threatened by negative thoughts and low self-esteem. The healing energy of self-care is soothing and gentle, and it empowers us with self-love so we can return to our daily activities more confident and grounded.

With self-care tools and techniques, we can generate mindfulness within ourselves and use the gift of deep breathing when we are exposed to discomfort. We learn how to breathe, invite different self-care tools, and find refuge inward without feeding on unnecessary stimulants and distractions. It is a well-rounded and complete self-support system in times of need.

Self-care will never threaten, betray, or abandon us when we need support, healing, and love. It is truly unconditional and generously giving. Letting self-care into our lives is the best action we can take to receive constant emotional support, mentorship, and wisdom from our higher selves.

How long does it take to feel the benefits of self-care?

There is no set timeline to learn how to connect with our emotions and sensations through self-care. Our practice should focus on gradually uncovering our authentic selves and slowly arriving at a better understanding of our feelings. The patience and commitment we invest in our wellness practice will naturally reward us with enhanced awareness and conscious realizations.

What if we don't know how to do self-care?

We might at first perceive self-care as selfish and wellness to be overly demanding. This feeling will eventually transform into self-empathy and serve as our source of confidence, empowerment, and courage. The initial fear and doubt also teach us the valuable lesson of how to prepare for greater growth. It is okay to let these thoughts be present as we transition from one stage of our lives to another in positive directions.

How do we practice self-care?

We can first explore different wellness tools and self-care techniques to see if they can be incorporated into our schedule. Some options include journaling, meditation, breathing exercises, physical exercise, prayer, self-massage, and in-depth tools like talk therapy, Emotional Freedom Technique (EFT) tapping, progressive muscle relaxation (PMR), mindfulness-based stress reduction (MBSR), and others.

The next step is to apply it into practice and carefully observe our comfort level regarding compatibility and practicality. We can then begin to create a long-term self-care and wellness routine incorporating the most effective tools and other positive daily habits.

We can step out of our comfort zone during the initial stages and experiment further with various methods, but the final objective is to dedicate our energy to building a more established and grounded practice we can regularly rely on and draw inspiration from.

Can self-care help overcome anger, frustration, depression, and anxiety?

It is natural to feel negative emotions and to witness others harboring internal suffering. To cope and maneuver mindfully, it is essential to actively release repressed emotions through wellness before reaching an emotional breakdown.

Repressed feelings need careful attention and observation to neutralize their intensity and lessen the ego attachments. We must monitor our thoughts, feelings, and sensations daily to protect our dear ones and ourselves from violent speech and toxic energy.

How do we cope with everyday stress through self-care?

It's easy to return to the habit of using unhealthy entertainment and stimulants to destress. But this is only a short-term method of distracting ourselves from suffering through dependence on artificial pleasure. It is not a long-term solution or a remedy to exhaustion and mental unease.

Instead of cycling through toxic habits in unproductive ways, we need to invite wellness into our routine to release accumulated tension and unease. We can begin with practicing self-care to dissolve negative energy and channel our stress correctly.

Does self-care promote emotional awareness?

Emotional awareness is the power to be receptive to our emotions and sensations with mindfulness. We form a profound connection with our inner being and further understand our true needs, motivations, and hidden desires in a safe and nonjudgmental environment.

It is an essential tool in helping us uncover our memories, past trauma, attachments, and belief systems that shape our current experiences. It is an antidote to repressed emotions, self-rejection, and unconscious destructive behaviors.

How does taking care of our emotions improve our overall life?

Taking time to care for our emotions through wellness allows us to deliberately channel our energy into things we want to nurture and amplify. It gives us the freedom to decide which good feelings we want to grow dominant through inner work. Our guidance and wisdom come from the intuitive knowledge of our higher selves and our deeper emotions.

Overall, we become more neutral and nonavoidant to challenging situations and people outside our control. We no longer depend on the selfish need to blame, guilt-trap, negatively project, deflect responsibility, or be passive-aggressive. We live as our new and improved selves without feeling confused and overwhelmed by our emotional complexities.

Is it possible to stop feeling negative emotions?

Negative emotions help us facilitate further learning and understanding of human tendencies. They are useful in allowing us the diverse experience of contrast, creativity, and limitless possibilities. Without them, we will not have the necessary tools to survive in a complex environment.

We don't necessarily have to stop feeling negative emotions or feel hatred for our natural traits. We can allow these sensations and feelings to be present without being overly attached and triggered. As wellness practitioners, we have to be mindful of not dramatizing and exaggerating pure emotions with self-created illusions. We can make friends with our negative emotions without altogether rejecting them.

Why is it our responsibility to practice wellness?

Being a responsible practitioner means taking care of our emotions and stress through healing techniques, including wellness and mindfulness. If we exclude these essential practices, we inevitably give birth to negative projections and toxic behavioral patterns. We become susceptible to engaging in arguments, violent forms of communication, and judging others. We fall into forgetfulness, resulting in mindless consumption, toxic habits, and self-destructive patterns.

Our responsibility and duty are to spread loving energy to our surroundings by, first and foremost, caring for our inner selves. Our positive presence can have a significant impact on those we care about and cherish. Long-term commitment to any methods of self-love will restore harmony and repair the loss of connection among all living beings.

GET TO KNOW YOURSELF

When is the last time you took a moment to reflect on your traits, tendencies, preferences, and emotional makeup? Invite the practice of self-awareness into your first wellness practice.

- What is your name?

- What are your physical features?

- What kind of person do you consider yourself to be?

- What do you love in life?

- When are you most joyous?

- Who is the person you love and cherish the most besides yourself?

- What are your life values?

- What's the best part of being you?

- What are your beliefs in life?

- What do you have faith in?

- Where do you love visiting?

- What's your favorite book?

- What's your favorite quote or saying?

- What's the best decision you made in life?

- What's something you never regret?

- What's one bold move you made in life?

- What do you enjoy eating?

- How does living in your personal space feel?

- What is your most prized possession?

- Who is the one who knows most about you besides yourself?

- What do your friends help you with?

- What kind of people do you enjoy talking to the most?

- What do your family members help you with?

- What's the most important thing in life?

- What are you good at?

- What's your unique gift or talent?

- What have you been complimented on?

- What's your favorite body part or facial feature?

- When do you feel attractive?

- When and how do you express generosity?

- What do you usually compliment others on?

- When do you thank others?

- When do you feel most confident?

- When are you most productive?

- When do you feel most rested and comfortable?

- What's something you are unconventional in?

- What's the easiest thing in life?

- How do you describe your personality?

- What are you most inspired by?

- What do you say to encourage yourself?

- What's the most important thing in your current life?

- What is your life's purpose?

- What's something you always wanted to try?

- Overall, what kind of person are you?

EMOTIONAL MAKEUP

Observing the fluctuations and patterns in our emotions allows us to be mindful of how we feel throughout the day and in general. Practicing awareness of our feelings enables us to connect with our deepest selves.

- How do you usually feel in the morning?

- How do you usually feel throughout the day?

- How do you usually feel before going to bed?

- Do you consider yourself an overall positive, negative, or neutral person, or a mixture of diverse traits?

- List five emotions you consider to be positive.

- List five emotions you consider to be negative.

- Who or what makes you feel positive?

- Who or what makes you feel negative?

- How would you like to feel?

- How would you not like to feel?

NEGATIVE VERSUS POSITIVE HABITS

Looking deeply at our habits and daily rituals empowers us in our journey of self-awareness. We can discover our honest thoughts and feelings toward the actions we take, both consciously and unconsciously. Take a moment to reflect on any habits that resonate negatively or positively.

STEP 1

Designate a day to carefully observe your negative habits. Take note of what you do repeatedly and consistently. Write what you notice about your behavior patterns on a notepad or journal, or make a mental note.

STEP 2

On another day, do the same thing, but this time, observe your positive habits. Take note of what you do repeatedly and consistently.

STEP 3

Compare the negative and positive habits and see which is more dominant. Focus on honest reflection without self-criticism or judgment.

STEP 4

Practice journaling or contemplation about what you would like to nourish more to help dissolve negative habits. See if there is a way to balance the unwanted behaviors with more proper nourishments.

WELLNESS SELF-ASSESSMENT

You can understand your current approach and capacity by assessing your self-care practice. Where are you now in terms of actively releasing stress and nurturing your inner self through proper nourishments? Use the guide below to assign a value to each point, then add up the total.

How often do you do these practices?

4: frequently
3: occasionally
2: rarely
1: never

Physical

eat regularly

hydrate regularly

eat mostly what you consider healthy and nutritionally balanced

eat fresh and mostly unprocessed foods

care for your skin, hair, and nails

participate in physical activities or regular exercise

do something relaxing: hot baths, yoga, massage

get professional medical care or seek helpful health-related resources when needed

get enough good-quality sleep

consciously limit the use of electronic devices when not needed

take time off when you are sick

take it easy when you notice cold, allergy, or flu symptoms starting

take day trips, vacation, or holidays

wear clothes and shoes you like

clean and tidy your space

Mental

write or express your feelings

read books for leisure

try or learn something new

meditate or contemplate on deep thoughts

receive support from courses, coaching, mentorship, counseling, trustworthy friends

say no when you want to

stick with your intuition or gut feelings

know when you are stressed

take action to reduce stress

voice your thoughts and opinions

challenge old beliefs

be mindful of yourself and your surroundings: other living beings and the Earth

walk away from negative influences offline and online

channel anger in a constructive and nonviolent way

practice nonviolent ways of communicating

Spiritual

go into nature

make time for prayer, meditation, affirmations, or self-reflections

participate in spiritual gatherings, communal meet-ups, or public get-togethers

be open to mystery and not knowing things

sing or listen to inspiring music

notice small things to feel appreciative about

express gratitude and thank others

practice generosity through donations, sharing, giving, and helping

celebrate the good things in life

express love toward dear ones

contemplate the meaning of life

believe that things will get better

surrender when things are uncontrollable

experiment with consciousness expansion

spend time with animals, plants, and insects

SCORE

140–180: You practice self-care consistently.

99–139: You practice self-care most of the time.

58–98: You practice self-care rarely.

below 45: Self-care doesn't seem to be a part of your life yet.

LIFE ENERGY BALANCE

Where do you invest and channel most of your energy? These prompts are designed to provide the clarity of knowing what you enjoy the most, what you feel obligated to do, and what you tend to avoid due to stress or discomfort.

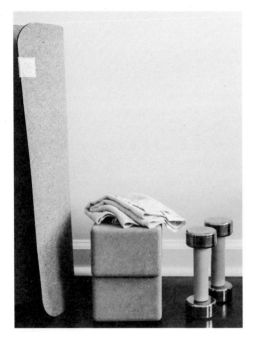

- Which activities do you like to spend energy on?

- What are things you feel obligated to spend energy on?

- Which activities drain you the most?

- Which activities replenish your energy?

- In which areas can you spend less energy?

- When do you feel most refreshed?

- When do you feel most energetic?

- What are things you have been avoiding lately?

- How does stress affect your energy level?

- What is one thing you do unconsciously that may decrease your energy?

- What percentage of the day do you feel low in energy?

- When was the last time you felt a steady flow of energy?

- In the past year, did your energy level increase or decrease?

- Did anything change in that time?

WELLNESS VISION BOARD

Creating a collage of your vision can help you specify your goals and desired manifestations. You can focus on visualizing how you want to feel, what your life will look like, what aesthetics you are drawn to, and what emotions your wellness routine and self-care practice will evoke. Let's dive into manifestation through powerful imagination in this guided exercise.

STEP 1

Prepare a sheet of paper, board, or digital device where you can make your collage. Set it aside for now.

STEP 2

Sit in a comfortable place where you feel relaxed and at ease.

STEP 3

Close your eyes and settle into a comfortable sitting or lying position.

STEP 4

Invite the thought of your ideal lifestyle centered on wellness, self-care, and positive nourishments. Think deeper about the details, including your morning routine, nighttime routine, self-care rituals, and the kind of lifestyle you will live as an emotionally, physically, and mentally stable person.

STEP 5

Keep imagining and take notice of the feeling you have when you're imagining living the life you want. Continue for at least ten minutes.

STEP 6

When ready, open your eyes to transfer your imagined thoughts onto paper or a digital presentation. Create a collage of your imagined thoughts. Be sure to include images, colors, quotes, or any visual representation of your ideal lifestyle or desired self-care routine.

THE FIVE NOURISHMENTS

We can now take time to lay down the foundations for the tools we will begin to incorporate in our self-care routine. Let's start the brainstorming process to actualize a wellness-oriented lifestyle.

Diet and Health

- What do you enjoy eating the most for breakfast?

- What do you enjoy eating the most for lunch?

- What do you enjoy eating the most for snacks?

- Which food feels best for your digestion and stomach?

- What do you enjoy eating the most for dinner?

- What do you enjoy drinking the most?

- How many meals do you like to eat in a day?

- How much water do you like to drink in a day?

- What are your current goals in diet, health, and well-being?

Education and Entertainment

- What do you want to read in the next six months?

- What do you want to watch in the next six months?

- What do you like to do to entertain yourself?

- How would you like to nourish your mind and educate yourself?

- What are your current goals in self-education and the ways you find entertainment?

Human Connection and Relationships

- Who do you enjoy being with the most?

- Who is most supportive in your family?

- What is one activity you like to engage in with others?

- What are your current goals in human connection, social life, and relationships?

Work, Hobbies, and Creativity

- What do you enjoy doing as a hobby?

- Which activities nurture creativity within you?

- When is the best time to work?

- What are your current goals in work, hobbies, and creativity?

Rest

- What's your favorite way to rest?

- Which day of the week do you like to rest?

- When is the best time of the day to rest?

- Do you like to do any activities to help you relax while resting?

- How long do you like to spend resting?

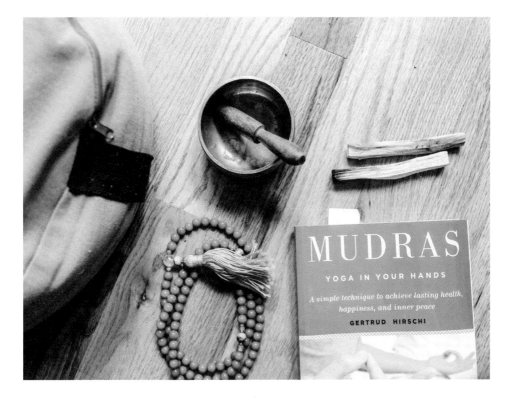

SELF-LEARNING REPORT

Now is a good moment to facilitate self-learning and decide which specific self-care methods and activities are preferred and most appropriate for you. Be open to exploring new approaches and learning from your personal studies and experimentation.

- What are some self-care activities you have already tried or are currently doing?

- Do you prefer active or sedentary self-care practices?

- Choose a maximum of five practices that sound interesting to you:

meditation

prayer

reflective journaling

breathing exercises

affirmations

mudras

sound baths

energy healing

chanting or singing

acupressure

guided visualization

pranic healing

Reiki

aromatherapy

crystal healing

astrology

Emotional Freedom Technique (EFT) tapping

progressive muscle relaxation (PMR)

mindfulness-based stress reduction (MBSR)

body scan meditation

yoga

tai chi and qi gong

physical exercise

massage

talk therapy

forest bathing

nature walks

religious studies

creating art

musical practice

- Do you have any other self-care practices you want to try that are not included? If there is a practice you are not yet familiar with, search the Web or refer to books to write a summary of each practice. Include what it is, the different options it has, how it works, and any other details.

- Which practice would you like to try first?

- What's most appealing about this particular self-care practice?

- Do you need any additional props?

- When is the earliest you can start?

EASY SELF-CARE LIST

Feel free to explore any additional fun and playful activities to nourish yourself. Pick activities that are lighthearted and less structured compared to the choices from the previous section.

Do gentle stretching.

Walk barefoot.

Go for a light walk.

Swing on a tree.

Balance on something.

Hang on something.

Clean or organize your space.

Turn off notifications.

Chew your food slowly.

Spend time with animals.

Spend time with someone positive.

Make a vision board.

Do something that makes you laugh.

Take a hot bath or shower.

Visit a spa.

Read.

Cook at home.

Sing out loud.

Doodle.

Drink tea.

Chat with someone.

Listen to music.

Watch a movie or a video.

Light a candle.

Take a nap.

Decorate your space with flowers.

Go sunbathing.

Care for your houseplants.

Snuggle in bed.

Wear something comfortable and cozy.

Do a face mask.

Go for a hike.

Go swimming.

Go to a farmers market.

Ride a bike.

Play a nourishing game.

Make lemonade or your favorite drink.

Repair something.

Plan a vacation or trip.

Go to bed early.

Give hugs.

Brush your hair or body.

Do your skin care routine.

Watch the sunset or sunrise.

Listen to motivational talks or podcasts.

Eat more plants, vegetables, and fruits.

Write a kind letter to someone.

Visit your favorite place.

Attend a meet-up.

Share your secret with someone special.

Donate something.

Do gardening.

Compliment yourself in the mirror.

Say yes to a new opportunity.

SELF-CARE PLANNER

We are ready to align with our practice through daily or regular commitments. Let's plan and specify the time to practice self-care. Feel free to use the planner below to create a general outline. You don't have to follow the same schedule all the time as things may change. Remember to be flexible and open.

- What time of the day do you have the most energy and motivation?

- Do you prefer morning self-care, midday self-care, nighttime self-care, or a combination?

- How much time do you have in the day to practice self-care?

- How frequently do you want to do each self-care practice?

- Would you like to include any rest days to skip self-care?

- What is one motivational affirmation or reminder you would like to remember?

- What is one self-love reminder you would like to remember?

- What is one self-worth reminder you would like to remember?

- What is one self-empowerment reminder you like to remember?

- What is one positive reminder you would like to remember when you forget to do self-care or don't have time?

INNER SACRED SPACE

Open a journal, notepad, or digital device to write down any further thoughts, feelings, and realizations uncovered during self-care practice in the past days or months. You can express yourself without limits and liberate your inner being from the fear of judgment. This is a safe place for you to open your heart. Don't be afraid to dive deeper and share your hidden desires, needs, and wants.

Feel free to explore some of these questions as a guide.

- How do you feel right now?

- What have you been craving lately?

- What do you feel grateful for?

- What brought you joy today?

- What made you feel down lately?

- What made you frustrated this week?

- What made you smile this week?

- What do you want to heal within yourself?

- How satisfied are you with your current lifestyle, routine, and habits?

SHADOW WORK JOURNALING

Shadow work was conceived by psychologist Carl Jung and focuses on working through our emotions and mental constructs to embrace negative thought patterns, feelings, and sensations through neutral acceptance.

Sometimes self-care practices and the moments we invite stillness reveal undiscovered thoughts and hidden feelings. You may now begin to notice unaddressed emotions and traits that you want to change or disown. If that happens, this may be a good time to invite shadow work to process what was repressed before your commitment to self-care.

- Did self-care help you discover or become aware of any negative traits and emotions that have bothered you?

- What is the most difficult emotion to handle in your current life?

- What is the most undesirable trait within you?

- Do you ever lie to others to hide your true feelings? If so, what are you hiding?

- Do you see anyone in your family or circle of friends who has similar undesirable traits?

- What is the most unforgivable thing a person could do to you?

- If you could erase a memory, what would you like to forget?

- How would you be different by not having those memories?

- Was there anyone who hurt your feelings in your life?

- What did they do to trigger you?

- What part of this person is most unlikeable or harmful? Are they lazy, lame, unproductive, irresponsible, egotistic, arrogant, hypocritical?

- Why do you think they chose to behave that way?

- What kind of emotional struggles were they projecting onto you?

- Do you believe you can also hurt others if you are struggling with similar feelings or situations as this person?

- Thinking of examples, what are some similarities between you two?

- What do you think this person needed the most help with not to behave negatively?

- How can this person improve their life to be a better person?

- What are some things you learned from this experience?

- Do you believe having emotions and being able to feel are important experiences? If so, why?

- What are parts of yourself you have neglected that you can start embracing?

POSITIVE SELF-TALK

Knowing our shadows and hidden traits gives us the power to transform them and shed healing light through positive self-talk. Today, we can invite the light of positivity as a part of our self-care practice to dissolve stress, difficult emotions, and mental blocks.

STEP 1

Find a comfortable and safe place where you can be alone. Take a seat in a posture that makes you feel at ease.

STEP 2

Recall any stress triggers, emotional struggles, negative thoughts, or specific shadow traits you want to dissolve. Take notice of the feelings and bodily sensations that arise from allowing them to resurface.

STEP 3

Transition from the thought by inviting a positive affirmation over the negative energy. Below are some examples to guide you.

NEGATIVE THOUGHT

"I am too sensitive and anxious."

"I am always angry, and I hate it."

"I hate parts of my life."

POSITIVE AFFIRMATION

"My sensitivity is my strength. It's what makes me unique."

"My anger protects me, and I know how to use it in a positive way."

"Everything is working out for me in life even though it is not always perfect."

STEP 4

Open your eyes once you have repeated the affirmation at least a couple of times. See if you feel any shifts or lightheartedness within. Repeat this practice two more times within a week or whenever you feel the same negative patterns rising. Feel free to make this your daily positive affirmation and a part of your emotional self-care. You can focus on different triggers, topics, or feelings and thoughts relevant to you in that moment.

LETTER TO OUR INNER CHILD

Work with our inner child is an important part of emotional self-care. Inner child work originates from psychologist Carl Jung's practice on healing the internal child archetype. Our inner child is an unconscious subpersonality linked to learned experiences in the early years of our lives. Healing the child within means restoring a state of innocence and purity by dissolving trauma and emotional wounds.

If we could return to our innocent child selves, how would we treat them and help them realize how precious and worthy they truly are? Write a letter to your inner child in a compassionate and loving voice. Let them know they are held dear.

CREATIVE SELF-CARE

Processing our emotions and thoughts through making art can be a nourishing self-care activity. The purpose of using art as a therapeutic healing exercise is to experiment with abstract feelings in an unfiltered and natural way. You can focus less on making what is aesthetically pleasing or beautiful; your creation can be entirely conceptual, spontaneous, and free-spirited.

STEP 1

To begin, prepare a sheet of paper and a set of markers, colored pencils, crayons, paste, watercolors, or any medium of your choice. Using a color medium is recommended because colors are directly connected to our emotions and can help us express ourselves fully.

STEP 2

Take a moment to invite the breath. Feel free to close your eyes while inhaling and exhaling deeply three times.

STEP 3

While continuing to breathe with awareness, take a moment to recall any dominant emotions you felt this week. What's been bothering you? You can also recall positive emotions if they were more dominant.

STEP 4

Allow what was felt to transfer onto paper by freely creating lines, shapes, and drawings. Let it flow and be known in a physical way.

STEP 5

Take a moment to invite reflection when you have completed the art. Gather a writing tool or digital device to journal while observing your finished work. Answer the following prompts.

- How did you feel while making the art?

- What kind of thoughts and feelings came up afterward?

- Does the artwork remind you of anything? If so, describe what it is and how it is related to your life.

SELF-LOVE JAR

Sometimes we fill our inner world with thoughts and feelings that no longer serve us. We often worry about our future, politics, social problems, and personal challenges. This can all lead us to direct negative self-talk directed at ourselves. Let's dissolve the energy of worry and pessimism by filling our hearts with soothing self-love reminders.

STEP 1

Prepare an empty jar or bowl, pencil, scissors, and paper.

STEP 2

Write at least ten compassionate notes to yourself and cut them into squares small enough to fit into the jar. Feel free to add drawings if you want to be creative. Examples:

- I am exactly where I want to be right now.

- I love how exciting and diverse my life is.

- I appreciate the imperfections in life.

- I love myself as I am, even if I face challenges.

STEP 3

Place all the self-love reminders in the jar. Leave the jar in a sacred place where you will see it when you get up in the morning. Let it stay there overnight to gather loving energy.

STEP 4

Take a moment the next morning to visit the jar and randomly pick one self-love reminder.

STEP 5

Place the note in your pocket, bag, wallet, or anywhere convenient near your body. Carry the reminder with you throughout the day and refer to it whenever you feel the need for gentle reminders.

Repeat for two consecutive days or as long as you want.

WORD OF APPRECIATION

Let's praise ourselves for following through on our self-care and wellness practice. We have all worked together to create this atmosphere of loving-kindness toward ourselves and those around us. We now are more aligned than ever to the path of loving our whole selves, including our mind, body, and soul.

Now is a good time to invite words of appreciation, gratitude, and praise to celebrate your progress. Feel free to engage in any physical way to express how proud you feel. Some ideas:

- Give yourself a hug.

- Ask for a hug from someone you want to share your joy with.

- Reward yourself with a day off from self-care or planned activities.

- Consume nourishment.

FIFTEEN-DAY SELF-CARE JOURNALING CHALLENGE

We can wrap up the final section of the wellness guide with a pat on the back! If you are up for another challenge, you can also bring closure with a fifteen-day self-care journaling challenge. Join us for two full weeks to deepen your practice of self-reflection and self-awareness. Invite any writing tool, and let's begin.

PREP DAY	DAY 1	DAY 2	DAY 3
Choose your sacred journal and writing tool to prepare.	Write ten things you are grateful for.	List relaxing things you did today.	Do a mind, body, and soul check-in. Write how you feel.
DAY 4	**DAY 5**	**DAY 6**	**DAY 7**
Reflect on what you were stressed about and what you did in reaction.	Write about a challenge you overcame and how you did it.	Write about your favorite place and why you love it.	Do a review of a book that inspired you.
DAY 8	**DAY 9**	**DAY 10**	**DAY 11**
List three people you appreciate and why you feel grateful to be a part of their lives.	Reflect on your greater purpose and what you would like to do in this time on Earth.	List fifteen things you do for fun.	Write about the lessons you learned this year.
DAY 12	**DAY 13**	**DAY 14**	**DAY 15**
Write about a time you felt stress-free.	List five ways you can feel more empowered.	Write why you are most important in your life.	Write your definition of health, happiness, and peace.

MINDFULNESS

What is mindfulness?

Mindfulness is the practice of awakening to the present moment through conscious awareness and deep understanding. Being mindful draws us inward to reflect on our thoughts, emotions, and sensations indiscriminately, without resistance or attaching judgment. When we invite mindfulness and its supportive practices, including sitting meditation and deep breathing, we begin to notice and accept life situations without wanting to change them, but accept them as natural unfoldings. We become more peaceful and less reactive by returning to a harmonious state through observation, self-reflection, and contemplation. We can learn how to be more mindful within our daily lives by carrying out the energy of mindfulness and engaging in wholesome activities through walking meditation, mindful speech, mindful listening, mindful eating, work meditation, and mindful sharing. The resulting benefit of daily practice can help us better manage stress, life challenges, and unpleasant feelings.

Why is mindfulness important?

Mindfulness is essential in restoring right-mindedness to the self and to human consciousness. Being without the practice of mindfulness or any other similar disciplinary practice can result in the creation of mindless energy and perpetual confusion. Living mindlessly can lead to acts of self-sabotage and harm against those around us, as we are unaware of the consequences of our actions and the meaning behind our intention. Mindfulness plays a crucial role in overcoming the absence of mind and forgetfulness. It allows us to feel stable, faithful, and grounded when exposed to distractions and external sources that may lead to temporary confusion.

What are the benefits of becoming mindful?

Once we begin, we will experience powerful insights and wisdom we have never accessed. Our actions, words, expression, and beingness will effortlessly stem from mindful energy. Growth and expansion will occur in all areas of life, raising our consciousness and improving our life experience as a peaceful person. We will gradually mature as practitioners capable of holding spaciousness at times of difficulty, challenges, and life's obstacles. Continuous mental discipline and training through active mindfulness and mindfulness-based tools will result in feeling more patient and calm and less prone to being reactive.

Who can practice mindfulness?

Everyone can incorporate mindfulness in their daily routine. It is not necessary to have a background in meditation or disciplined practice. No one is excluded from the joy of breathing and inviting peace within.

What Is the purpose of breathing mindfully?

Mindfulness promotes the quality of breath and focuses on its importance through daily practice. Breathing without mindful awareness can cause reckless, impulsive, and rash behavior stemming from forgetfulness. That is why it is necessary to monitor the breath during our practice to bring serenity and return to the peace of our inner temple. We can gently correct labored and strenuous breathing and dissolve the state of restlessness, agitation, and frustration by inhaling and exhaling profoundly. We can take as much time as we need, being patient with ourselves to steady the breath, slow the heartbeat, and release the momentum of rushing and doing. Our daily practice can remind us to invite mindful breathing when we rise in the morning, drink tea, eat our meals, have conversations, and engage in life's work and duties.

Why did you become a practitioner of mindfulness?

My daily practice became an important part of my life because I desired a gentle way to dissolve my past habits, transform my attachments, and dissolve suffering. It has been my way of dissolving inner pain by seeing the present and not being stuck in the past. I thought that many of the difficulties I faced as an adult, including negative physical symptoms, emotional burdens, and mental attachments, could stem from the continuation of what I learned in childhood and the unresolved issues passed down from my ancestors. My obsession with hoarding and my shopping addiction felt directly related to the scarcity mind-set I observed when I was a child. As I grew older and became emotionally and mentally ready to mature, I felt a strong desire to cultivate freedom from all the learned patterns and personal history holding me back.

Did you become more mindful after practice?

After seven years, mindfulness continues to guide my attention in a wholesome direction, away from old attachments. It corrects my ego's need to dwell in negativity by dissolving the justification of past hardship. I see the unfolding of my journey with more right-mindedness and neutrality, although this is not always available. I feel more willing to forgive than ever before, more open to letting go of the assumptions and attachments I held onto, and more

ready to transform my inner world through the light of compassion and consciousness. What remains for me is continuous practice as I experience growth.

How does mindfulness work?

Mindfulness is the practice of bringing back awareness of our mind, body, and surroundings. We invite the energy of mindfulness and work on being fully attentive to the present moment through various methods, including deep breathing, contemplation, sitting meditation, and active mindfulness.

Why is the present moment important?

Being in the present moment means embracing the wonders of life entirely. We don't expend our precious energy worrying about the future, replaying past mistakes, obsessively planning, or being driven by anxious thoughts. We become available to the offerings of life's diversity and sources of joy without self-created mental formations and disturbances. When we dwell in the illusions outside the present moment, we can lose touch with what is real, feel confused, and be unable to see the beauty of life.

Does mindfulness improve mental health?

Mindfulness allows us to let go naturally through the cleansing energy that washes over our minds and emotions when we breathe deeply. It helps us recover from toxic thought patterns as it gently purges us of our attachment to self-created illusions and distractions. It restores our beingness to a state of purity and greater receptiveness to the miracles in front of us.

We become more expressive and open with our positive qualities, including patience, equanimity, generosity, kindness, understanding, and overall emotional intelligence. We bring forth the new and improved version of ourselves, spreading joy and health to all living beings.

When can we practice mindfulness?

We can practice mindfulness throughout the day, when we wash the dishes, tidy our space, exercise, commute, and all our routines and daily activities. We can carry the energy of gentleness and ease through deep breathing and full attention while engaged in other things.

When we eat, we can decide to invite mindfulness by chewing slowly and observing our food. We can also be attentive to our surroundings and our breath and movement when we are walking. There are many ways we can invite our practice without disrupting our rhythm. We can let mindfulness flow and be seamless.

Do we have to meditate to practice mindfulness?

Bringing meditation into our practice is an essential part of mindfulness. But we can decide which techniques and methods are most compatible for our unique needs. We can approach several paths, including sitting meditation, service meditation, walking meditation, resting meditation, movement meditation, and many more. Most important is sitting meditation, which also has several options to experiment with, including guided meditation, silent meditation, body scan meditation, Transcendental Meditation, and others.

The purpose of sitting meditation is to bring full attention back to our mind, body, and soul. Returning to our inner selves allows us to take time to let go of what is unreal to create spaciousness within. We no longer let passing thoughts and feelings dominate our moods and clutter our minds. We surrender and allow everything to be as it is. We recognize the presence of both the negatives and the positives by restoring neutrality and equanimity.

If any hesitation or doubt about inviting meditation rises, we can contemplate our resistance and give it more thought and observation. We can ask ourselves, Why are we fearful of stillness? Why are we worried about what we will uncover within ourselves? Perhaps we are scared of not doing it perfectly or performing our best. We can slowly dissolve our assumptions by learning what works for us along the way.

How do we know we are mindful enough?

If any doubt arises, remember where we were before our journey and the place we are currently standing. Notice any subtle physical, emotional, and mental benefits we have been experiencing so far. Have we been ignoring these beautiful unfoldings and expecting too much from ourselves? Return to honest reflection and look to things we can be grateful for instead of making abrupt changes or giving up.

The present moment is full of gifts, and we only have to take time to look at it with a mindful eye and an open heart. We can choose to take refuge in the reassurance of our daily commitments instead of superficially measuring our achievements. We can look to the core values and everyday practice for encouragement, self-confidence, and positive recognition. Being patient and steady is the key to mindfulness.

How long does it take to become mindful?

We can invite mindfulness whenever we begin our intentional practice through mindful breathing and other daily commitments. We can experience the positive shifts in our mind, body, and soul once we make the conscious decision to allow awareness to enter the present moment. It does not take much time for us to experience relaxation and more ease, but it does require discipline to feel consistently aligned with inner peace. We have to remember to practice regularly and unconditionally.

How can we be mindful in a modern world?

At first, it may be challenging to accommodate others and let others explore our practice. We may face temporary obstacles as we work on grounding ourselves in chaotic and hectic environments. It may be difficult to offer the energy of mindfulness to those resistant or unaware of our intentions.

But this is more reason to return to our breath and realign with our practice. We should bring harmony and peace to ourselves and the world by letting go of the barriers that hold us back from offering understanding, deep connection, and empathy. We need mindfulness more than ever to heal our brothers and sisters and all living beings from disconnection.

We can cultivate nondiscrimination, unconditional love, and compassion beyond physical separation and material differences through our daily practices. We must put in the work to protect ourselves and our dear ones from misunderstanding, jealousy, competition, resentment, and violence against one other.

Are we bad practitioners if we become angry, anxious, or sad?

Feeling the rise of unwanted emotions does not make us bad practitioners of the core values of mindfulness. We can let these feelings and sensations flow and dissolve naturally instead of obsessing to fix or eliminate parts of ourselves. It is necessary to invite honesty and humility by being aware of discomfort without judgment or excessive attachment.

The key is to be mindful of our feelings and to breathe through all our human experiences to let go of repressed emotions and the toxic pattern of self-rejection and self-hatred.

Can mindfulness remove suffering and hardships?

Mindfulness can transform suffering, but it is not aimed at removing it. We as practitioners should recognize that paradise is in the present moment. It is never at an unreachable place where particular conditions must manifest for us to experience or access it.

We do not need more material wealth or physical success to be comfortable and safe. We do not need artificial protections to guard ourselves against the threat of pain and suffering. There is nothing to pursue or do.

What we need is already provided, if we choose to see it through our spiritual eye and right perception. Our work is not to remove or avoid obstacles, hardships, and turmoil, but to accept this miraculous moment as a whole. We need to stop, breathe, and practice to observe what is here.

MINDFULNESS SELF-EVALUATION

Let's begin our practice by inviting mindful awareness of our habitual energy, patterns, and tendencies. Observe what triggers bodily tension and mental and emotional strain. See if you resonate with more than half of the traits outlined below.

- I try to stay busy to avoid stillness and silence.

- I put on loud music or videos when it feels too quiet.

- I think being in nature is boring.

- I prefer loud parties and big crowds instead of talking and sharing with a friend.

- I tend to look for stimulating and exciting content online.

- I need coffee or other stimulants to keep me going through the day.

- I find it difficult to feel calm and peaceful.

- I feel even more restless when I am told to relax.

- I tense up easily without noticing it.

- I tend to fidget and move a lot unintentionally.

- I find myself losing patience sometimes.

- I feel frustrated when others are slower.

- I tend to rush my daily tasks: eating, cleaning, exercising, working, walking.

- I often cause accidents or small mishaps because I am rushing.

- Others have told me to back off or allow them space.

- Not doing anything makes me feel unproductive.

- The most important thing in my life is work.

- My mind is often occupied with worry.

- I tend to be competitive and goal oriented.

- I sometimes feel overwhelmed by the pressure I put on myself.

- Others often point out things I never notice.

- I tend to numb myself when I am outside.

- I tend to ignore physical pain and bodily responses: hunger, soreness, tiredness.

- I often avoid profound thoughts and deep emotions.

- I feel uncomfortable talking about my feelings.

- I am often unable to pick up on emotional cues.

- I change the subject when others talk about their emotional struggles.

- I feel triggered by what others say or do.

- I say things without really meaning to say them.

- When talking with others, my thoughts tend to wander.

- I often talk over others instead of allowing them to finish.

- Some people think I criticize them too often.

- I tell people what to do instead of just listening to them.

SOLUTION-FOCUSED QUESTIONS

The following questions focus on expanding understanding of our thought process and aims to help us find solutions within. Visit these questions to cultivate better focus, clear-mindedness, awareness, and better understanding of the mind's tendencies.

- What does your ideal day look like?

- Which emotions will you feel?

- What thoughts and physical sensations need to be released for you to enjoy your ideal day?

- How can mindfulness help you let go of this?

- How will other people respond positively when you practice mindfulness?

- Who besides yourself will be most affected by your practice?

- How will you know you are being mindful?

- What small changes, if any, have you already made to get closer to this?

- If you have, how did you feel when you made that decision?

- What additional tools do you need to manifest your ideal day?

- Which mindfulness-based activity are you ready to try next?

- What motivational affirmation is going to help you in the process?

- What reminder will help you be gentle when you forget to be mindful or feel the need to pause?

STRESS-LEVEL EVALUATION

Knowing your overall stress level can help you understand the source of tension, anxious thoughts, and mental blocks. Invite a couple of deep breaths and dive inward with these questions.

- What is your breath like at the moment?

- How often during the day do you feel restless or impatient?

- Where on your body do you feel that stress gathers the most?

- What is one area of your life that is causing stress right now?

- Write down why it triggers stress.

- What are some habits you have that make the stress worse?

- What are the environmental factors that make the stress worse: loud noises, a competitive workplace, a chaotic city?

- When you are stressed, how do you react to unpleasant situations and people?

- When you are stressed, how do you usually act toward yourself and others?

- What is one activity you do that relieves stress?

- What are some kind words you can say to yourself when you are stressed?

MINDLESS ENERGY ANALYSIS

Let's take a moment to reflect honestly on how our patterned behaviors result in mindlessness. We can observe with a gentle eye to dissolve any self-criticism or judgment of ourselves when mindfulness is not fully available. The objective is to arrive at understanding the internal mechanism that is preventing conscious awareness and mindful intentions.

- When do you feel most mindless?

- What are you usually doing when you are unaware and unconscious of your actions?

- When do you feel most pressured?

- When do you feel most overwhelmed?

- When do you feel most distracted?

- When do you tend to rush the most?

- What do you think makes you forget important things?

- What triggers you to make more mistakes than you usually do?

- What do you feel anxious talking about?

- Does going to a particular place make you feel nervous and tense? If so, where?

- Does dealing with something cause uneasiness? If so, what is it?

- When are you least mindless and more in alignment with mindfulness?

- When do you notice yourself feeling most peaceful?

- When do you feel most grounded and safe?

- When are you most focused and clear-minded?

- When are you most productive in a healthy way?

- When and where do you feel most relaxed?

BREATHING THROUGH STRESS

Breathing with mindfulness allows us to slow down, release mental clutter, and let go of distracting thoughts. We become more aware of our deepest emotional needs and life priorities without feeling distracted, overwhelmed, and hyperstimulated by environmental stress and external influences.

STEP 1

Prepare writing materials and find a comfortable and safe place to practice.

STEP 2

Recall a stressful event that occurred recently. It can be challenges at work, in a relationship, family problems, or health or mind-set related blocks.

STEP 3

Take notice of your physical response when you think of this stressful situation. Write down what you notice about your body temperature, breathing, muscular tension, perspiration, and posture when recalling stress triggers.

STEP 4

Put down the writing tool and invite deep breathing. Inhale and exhale deeply and slowly without rushing. Do this three times, or continue for five minutes. Focus on your breath even if it may not be perfectly deep or steady.

STEP 5

Return to your writing tool and share whether you feel any difference before and after inviting the breath, in your body temperature, muscles, and level of tension.

STEP 6

Pick one word to describe how you feel right now compared to breathing without mindfulness.

STEP 7

Optionally, take time for self-learning about different breathing techniques and guided audio practices. Holotropic Breathwork, alternate nostril breathing, and 4-7-8 breathing are recommended to explore.

MINDFUL BODY SCAN

Let's invite the practice of mindful body scan to return to tranquility. We will learn how to open our senses and awareness to what is within and around us through the practice of nonresistance and openness. This activity will help dissolve the fear of silence and stillness in the absence of doingness.

STEP 1

Create a sacred place to sit or lie down. Bring a blanket or throw for cover if needed.

STEP 2

Use an alarm or meditation timer if needed. Set it to ten or fifteen minutes or longer. Optionally, choose a guided mindful body scan meditation online to help you.

STEP 3

When ready, without rushing, arrive in a meditative posture. Invite deep breathing. Breathe in and out mindfully and fully.

STEP 4

Now take time to do a mental scan of your entire body. Start from the crown of the head to the tip of the toes. Slowly move downward, noticing any sensations. Then expand outward by becoming aware of your surroundings. Focus on what sounds, smells, and other elements are within the space.

STEP 5

Once you are finished scanning, return to these prompts to share details of the experience and any sensations that surfaced.

- Did you notice any scents?

- Did you notice any sounds?

- Did you notice any taste in your mouth?

- Did you notice how the surface felt?

- Did you feel cold, hot, warm, or neutral?

- What was your hunger level?

- What was your level of thirst?

- Did you notice any tension, soreness, or discomfort in certain areas? If so, where?

- Did you notice any pain? If so, where?

- Where did you feel the lightest?

- Where did you feel the heaviest?

- What was different after you did the body scan?

NONRESISTANCE TRAINING

Resistance can give birth to harshness within and prevent mindful thoughts and feelings from settling in our mind and heart. Let's invite gentle corrections to align with a state of ease and neutral acceptance. This moment serves as a reminder that nonresistant thoughts nurture peace and calm within.

STEP 1

Prepare a writing tool and create a list of things you currently feel resistant about. You can follow the guide below.

- List three personality traits you hate in others.

- List one thing you don't approve of in your closest friend.

- List one thing you don't approve of in one of your family members.

- List three things you don't like about your culture.

- List three things you don't like about the society you live in.

- List one unpleasant thing that happened today or recently.

- List one thing that you feel is unfair.

- List three things you want to change in yourself that are undesirable.

- List one thing you don't like about your job or how you support yourself financially.

- List one thing you don't like about your lifestyle.

- List one thing you don't like about the neighborhood you live in.

- List one thing you don't like about your relationship.

- List one thing you don't want to deal with today or in the upcoming weeks.

STEP 2

Put away the writing tool to invite deep breathing by inhaling and exhaling with awareness.

STEP 3

Choose one affirmation from the list below to recite in silence or out loud. Continue mindful breathing while inviting the affirmation.

- I am willing to forgive, listen, and be open to all my brothers and sisters.

- We all are diverse, creative, and uniquely different in our methods.

- I hold respect for others because I also respect my own decisions.

- Loving myself is an act of loving others unconditionally.

- I am grateful to live in the excitement of contrast and diversity.

- My life is never boring because it is full of ups and downs and opportunities to learn.

NEUTRALITY PRACTICE

Sometimes wanting forced positivity to be present all the time can lead to denial of reality and the present moment. This can also occur when we hold attachment to see things as negative even if we were never personally harmed. Now is a good time to embrace what is unfolding in life as it is, without distracting mental formations. Let's return to willing and neutral acceptance of all.

STEP 1

Enter a room or a closed space. Sit in stillness while inviting deep inhalation and exhalation.

STEP 2

Observe an object within your surrounding space. It can be a cup, a pillow, a clock, a phone, or anything near you.

STEP 3

Recite out loud or in silence within: "I do not feel good or bad about this [name of object]. I feel neutral." Repeat with five more objects nearest to you.

STEP 4

Do the same exercise within your daily life whenever you notice judgment, criticism, and limited perception causing separation between you and what you are observing. The subject can be a thing, a person, a situation, or a circumstance.

You don't have to sit or be in an enclosed room when using this technique while engaging in daily activities, but it is recommended that wherever you are, you always invite three deep breaths before reciting the neutral statement.

Examples

"I do not feel good or bad about my neighbor's dog. I feel neutral."

"I do not feel good or bad about my boss. I feel neutral."

"I do not feel good or bad about my job. I feel neutral."

"I do not feel good or bad about being yelled at. I feel neutral."

"I do not feel good or bad about feeling anxious. I feel neutral."

"I do not feel good or bad about this outfit. I feel neutral."

"I do not feel good or bad about my body. I feel neutral."

IMPERMANENCE LESSON

Endless wanting, craving, and fixation on limited beliefs and aggregates can be a form of obsession and attachment. This can sometimes divert our attention from precious unfoldings in the present moment that can be missed if not carefully observed. Let's use the power of observation and right perception by seeing things as impermanent and inherently free from greed, possessiveness, and unwholesome dependence.

STEP 1

Prepare a writing tool or a photographic device. You can use your phone.

STEP 2

Venture outdoors in natural surroundings. You can choose a trail, a nearby park, or any place where you can observe nature.

STEP 3

Take note of the things you observe that are impermanent within your surroundings. Take a picture or write a list of what you see.

STEP 4

Take a moment to sit in stillness to reflect on how you feel when contemplating the cycle of birth and death.

- How do you feel observing nature?

- What makes nature and life beautiful?

- Do you feel different knowing that everything in life is impermanent?

- How do you feel about the impermanence of animals, insects, and plants?

- How do you feel about the impermanence of Mother Earth and the natural world?

- How do you feel about your own impermanence?

DRAW YOUR INNER PEACE

Productive visualization and deep contemplation can help us manifest a focused life centered on mindfulness. Use your mind's power to imagine the calm that is within and the peace that is unfolding gradually on your path through practice.

STEP 1

To begin, prepare a sheet of paper and a set of markers, colored pencils, crayons, paste, watercolors, or any medium of your choice. Using a color medium is recommended because colors are directly connected to our emotions and can help us express ourselves fully.

STEP 2

Take a moment to invite the breath. Feel free to close your eyes while inhaling and exhaling deeply three times.

STEP 3

While continuing to breathe with awareness, take a moment to visualize a place of peace.

Focus on how it feels to be stress-free and at ease while dwelling in this place. What images, textures, lines, colors, and shapes fill that space of complete tranquility?

STEP 4

Allow what you felt to transfer onto paper by freely creating lines, shapes, and drawings. Let it flow and be known in a physical way.

STEP 5

Invite a moment of reflection when you have completed the artwork. Gather a writing tool or digital device to practice journaling while observing your finished work. Answer the following prompts.

- How did you feel while making the art?

- What kind of thoughts and feelings came up afterward?

- Does the artwork remind you of anything? If so, describe what it is and how it is related to your life.

GARDEN OF COMPASSION

Offering compassion to yourself and to others is one of the most important services to give when cultivating mindfulness. Let's spread loving-kindness and peaceful energy to all living beings by participating in active generosity. You can begin planting seeds of compassion for humanity, animals, insects, plants, and Mother Earth.

STEP 1

Prepare a writing tool.

STEP 2

Create a list of kind acts you have done to assist others in need. Include any mindful offerings you made to your family, partner, friends, coworkers, neighbors, community, and living things around you.

Include the date, location, what you did, and a brief note about how you felt afterward.

STEP 3

Create a separate list of kind acts you received from others. Also include a brief note about how you felt to receive generosity and compassion from kind souls.

STEP 4

Continue with the list until you have written down five acts of kindness for each list. Take a moment to close your eyes to feel gratitude and appreciation for each one. Feel free to say thank you in silence.

BUILDING OUR INNER TEMPLE

The mindfulness-based prompts, exercises, and activities we have completed so far guide us to our next course: transferring our learnings into physical action and daily discipline. This is the most important step in making full practical use of our growth and progress. Begin the process of building your inner mindfulness temple by brainstorming daily mindfulness routines.

- What did you learn so far about mindfulness?

- What did you realize so far about your mind and thought patterns?

- Did you notice any better way of coping with everyday stress?

- Do you think living a mindful lifestyle is compatible with you in the long term?

- Would you like to practice meditation consistently? Why or why not?

- Would you like to practice mindful breathing regularly? Why or why not?

- Do you want to make any mindful changes to improve how you speak?

- Do you want to make any mindful changes to improve how you listen to others?

- Do you want to make any mindful changes to improve how you treat yourself?

- Do you want to make any mindful changes to improve how you treat others?

- Do you want to make any mindful changes to improve how you behave at work?

- Do you want to make any mindful changes to improve how you entertain yourself?

- Do you want to make any mindful changes to improve how you consume?

- Do you want to make any mindful changes to improve how you deal with your emotions?

- Do you want to make any mindful changes to improve how you take care of your mental health?

- List five actions you want to take to be more mindful in your life.

- What is the first action you want to commit to?

- If you are not already doing so, when can you start more consistently practicing mindfulness-based techniques, including meditation, breathing, and other practice?

MINDFUL REST

We have arrived at the final section of the mindfulness workbook. Now is the right moment to reward yourself with a lazy day to practice resting meditation. Doing nothing and practicing nonstriving is also an essential part of our practice.

We have spent a lot of energy and invested precious time in personal development and spiritual studies through this workbook, so it is good to let the benefits of that discipline sink deep into our core. Half our work is consistent practice, and the other half is allowing the mind, body, and soul to absorb the positive effects. These methods of balancing and approaching things in moderation shape our routines into fruitful and nurturing practices. We become more grounded in our practices without neglecting our need for breaks, laziness, and ease. Being rested and calm is the most productive way to spend our day after hard work.

Let's give ourselves the gift of rest and relaxation for the work and practice we have been building. Doing nothing is part of our practice of letting go and healing.

SEVEN-DAY ACTIVE MINDFULNESS CHALLENGE

A seven-day active mindfulness challenge can allow us to find joy in the powerful healing effects of consecutive practice. Feel free to cultivate more awareness and groundedness through peaceful and relaxing mindfulness-based activities and meditation.

You can incorporate different techniques daily to explore various methods of cultivating inner calm. You can experience better focus, heightened perception of your emotions, more understanding of others, and a deeper appreciation for your breath and the miracle of life.

When ready, first set your intention to practicing and begin your first day with openness. Write your intention in your journal, on a sheet of paper, or on a digital device.

Day 1: Mindful Listening

OBJECTIVE

We spend our time rushing and going from one place to another, forgetting to sit in stillness to listen deeply. We deprive others of their need to share, express, and be heard in a loving and empathetic way. Even when we pause to offer our listening ear, we often distract ourselves with wandering thoughts and end up interrupting or misinterpreting the other person.

We need to return to mindful listening to hear what others truly want to convey and express. We must be available for our brothers and sisters to lift their suffering and pain.

Let's be of service to others by being generous with our time, presence, and attention.

STEPS

1. When you know you will be conversing with someone, clear your schedule, and make room for mindful communication.

2. If you have important matters to take care of, do it before you engage in the conversation. Let the other person know you will be fully available afterward.

3. Once you are in the same space with the other person or have the other person on the phone, direct your full attention to them.

4. Let them speak without interrupting or making remarks.

5. Focus on empathizing with their situation and refrain from giving unsolicited advice.

REFLECTION

Write how you felt and what difference it made in your life.

Day 2: Mindful Speech

OBJECTIVE

Being selective and mindful of our words allows the listener to feel safe. We must include mindful speech into our daily practice to restore nonviolence in our way of thinking, communicating, and sharing. Let's direct our energy toward good intentions by filling everyone's time and space with fruitful conversations.

If we choose to interrupt silence, we must do so mindfully and carefully.

STEPS

1. Choose words that spark positive feelings in yourself and others.

2. Be selective of what you say, and take your time to be selective instead of wanting to fill silence or gaps with unnecessary words.

3. Focus on sharing what is helpful, informative, and compassionate.

4. Speak to be honest and truthful and avoid contributing to narrow-mindedness, discrimination, violence, and false news.

5. Share from real experience stemming from your personal journey.

6. Be observant of the body language and energy you are projecting.

7. Pause and breathe if the other person is feeling uncomfortable about what you are saying. Give them the chance to create space or boundaries if they feel the need to withdraw.

8. Refrain from sharing with others and return to your practice of self-reflection when the need rises to judge, criticize, or feed into negative thoughts through ranting.

REFLECTION

Write how you felt and what difference it made in your life.

Day 3: Mindful Eating

Sometimes the energy of rushing can shape the way we prepare, cook, eat, and clean up after our meals. We may catch ourselves swallowing without chewing, overly stuffing our stomach, eating only to distract away from hardship, and putting food into the mouth robotically while mentally distracted about something else. It is an essential practice of mindfulness to dissolve mindless consumption and disorderly eating, including binging, overeating, and emotional eating through a healthy relationship with food and Earth's resources.

Let us invite mindfulness to properly transfer life-giving sources and nutrients to our body's core through optimal absorption, digestion, preparation, and conscious food choices.

STEPS

1. Gather what you know is nourishing, wholesome, and derived from compassionate sources. Do your groceries without buying in excess.

2. Prepare food to use each ingredient without waste. Think about the person who will eat it. Focus on transferring nurturing energy to yourself or the person who will consume what you prepare.

3. Serve the food with moderation in mind. Fill the dish with an appropriate portion. Not too much and not too little. Keep a side of extra (in moderate amounts) if you feel unsure and worry about undereating at first.

4. Before you eat, practice gratitude to the Earth and the resources used to create your meal through prayer or acknowledgment.

5. Observe the visuals of the food. See the shapes, colors, and textures. Remove all distractions if there's anything drawing your attention away from looking at your food.

6. Take a bite and be mindful of the taste and overall sensations.

7. Chew slowly and mindfully without rushing. You can try chewing thirty times.

8. Take your time, and once finished, recite another word of gratitude.

9. Clean the dishes immediately without letting them sit for later.

10. Wash the dishes without rushing, and focus on enjoying the process of cleaning and tidying up. Think of it as a light exercise to help you digest. In addition, you can invite a short walk to help with metabolism.

REFLECTION

Write how you felt and what difference it made in your life.

Day 4: Walking Meditation

OBJECTIVE

How often do we catch ourselves rushing and hurrying? It is rare for us to walk freely without holding onto thoughts of worry and distractions. We can release these mental blocks and restore a sense of lightheartedness whenever we walk mindfully. We can breathe through each step and let our bodies flow with the gentle rhythm of our inhalation and exhalation. Doing this as a part of our regular practice allows us to feel more peaceful and grounded in our bodies and wherever we arrive.

STEPS

1. Relax the tension in your neck, shoulders, arms, core, and legs. Carry yourself without being stiff and rigid.

2. Maintain good posture and walk without making any unnecessary movements.

3. Focus on landing your feet gently and deliberately without slamming them.

4. Alternate breaths every time you take two to three steps. Focus on flowing and synchronizing with the movement of your body.

5. Take notice of your bodily sensations, and be in the now with the surrounding elements.

6. Let go of the need to be somewhere, and be entirely present in the moment. Picture this moment and activity as the most important thing in the world.

REFLECTION

Write how you felt and what difference it made in your life.

Day 5: Service Meditation

OBJECTIVE

We can create mindfulness at work and during times of service by applying deep breathing. Practicing service meditation allows us to approach our work, business, career path, and contribution to our community with right-mindedness and positive intention. We learn how to nurture creativity, provide nourishment to our families, advance as a whole, and safely channel our energy and motivations.

STEPS

1. Choose to engage in work or activities that are nondestructive and nonviolent to other living beings.

2. Let uncontrollable elements in the surrounding environment be there, but make an effort to work productively without feeding on distractions and unnecessary noise.

3. Pay attention to your physical sensations and feelings while working and invite deep breathing to release stress or tension.

4. Notice your need for breaks and relaxation, and give yourself time to unwind.

5. Be sure not to get dehydrated or overwork yourself to the point of forgetting to eat or doing other essential tasks.

6. Practice gratitude and appreciation when you see the final results or any form of reward.

REFLECTION

Write how you felt and what difference it made in your life.

Day 6: Nature Meditation

OBJECTIVE

Restoring our bond with Mother Earth through nature meditation allows us to appreciate life and its miracles. The practice of breathing and walking in nature invites the cleansing and purifying energy of trees, plants, and air.

<u>STEPS</u>

1. Visit a place where natural elements such as trees and animals are abundant: a hiking trail, a park, a garden, or any other natural environment.

2. Be mindful of your surroundings while you stroll the path at a relaxed pace.

3. Observe the details of what you see by pausing to take notice of the things around you.

4. Breathe and invite fresh air into your inner self.

5. Help maintain the sacredness of where you are by picking up any trash you notice along the path.

6. Recite a word of gratitude within or out loud to Mother Earth before you decide to depart.

REFLECTION

Write how you felt and what difference it made in your life.

Day 7: Mindfulness Reminder

OBJECTIVE

We can create mindfulness at work and during times of service by applying deep breathing. Practicing service meditation allows us to approach our work, business, career path, and contribution to our community with right-mindedness and positive intention. We learn how to nurture creativity, provide nourishment to our families, advance as a whole, and safely channel our energy and motivations.

STEPS

1. Choose to engage in work or activities that are nondestructive and nonviolent to other living beings.

2. Let uncontrollable elements in the surrounding environment be there, but make an effort to work productively without feeding on distractions and unnecessary noise.

3. Pay attention to your physical sensations and feelings while working and invite deep breathing to release stress or tension.

4. Notice your need for breaks and relaxation, and give yourself time to unwind.

5. Be sure not to get dehydrated or overwork yourself to the point of forgetting to eat or doing other essential tasks.

6. Practice gratitude and appreciation when you see the final results or any form of reward.

REFLECTION

Write how you felt and what difference it made in your life.

MINDFUL CLOSURE

Our studies and practices within this guide come to a close. Use the questions below for final reflection to bring mindful closure without rushing to an end. This is a moment for us to invite gratitude for our progress, observe our transformation so far, and brainstorm what we wish to continue practicing.

- Which practice out of the four essential healing practices did you feel most eager to try?

- When did you first begin working with the guide?

- How were you then emotionally, mentally, and spiritually?

- What kind of lifestyle were you living?

- How are you now? Is there anything different after you became a conscious healer?

- What changes are you most proud of?

- What do you consider to be the most significant breakthrough?

- What are your current top priorities? Is it different from your past?

- What new beliefs do you now have?

- Do you feel informed and educated about mindfulness, sustainability, minimalism, or wellness?

- Are you comfortable with your current routines, habits, and practices?

- Is there anything you want to improve further in your lifestyle?

- Why is it important you continue improving that part of yourself?

- Imagine what you could achieve in one to five years. What kind of person will you be by continuing practicing at your current pace?

- Can you think of anyone you wish to share this guide and the light of healing with?

CONTINUOUS UNFOLDING

The power of healing through numerous benefits and positive manifestations will now be apparent to many of us. We are now steadily on the path of the desired stage of recovery, and we are better prepared than ever to maneuver mindfully and skillfully through the inevitable challenges of a diverse and contrasting environment. What we have cultivated so far through this guided experience will continue to create the momentum of further growth and broaden our inner potential. By witnessing more growth, we are always reminded that good things are already here, and more are always on the way.

How to Promote Healing Around Us

As we continue our path, we must remember that our actions, words, beliefs, and lifestyle choices significantly affect our surroundings and dear ones. For this reason, we must channel the learnings we have cultivated so far in positive directions. It is our responsibility to do good and actively take the lead to dissolve the contributors of negativity. That is the power we hold as informed healers and creators capable of necessary changes in ourselves and in others.

Our aim is to establish a meaningful practice we can actually make use of instead of choosing not to apply what we've learned to real life. The point is to promote healing in all of us instead of dwelling in separation or greed. It is always good to return to this understanding by using our wisdom and knowledge generously for the health and vitality of everyone. Let's not be afraid to do good for the purpose of healing the whole.

How to Heal the World

After completing the guide and establishing our routines, we may observe a lack of progress around us. We may view the distractions and surrounding chaos from our past environment as changeless despite our inner efforts. Witnessing old ways can come to us as unfair, threatening, and isolating, resulting in hostility against unchanging elements. Being out of touch with worldly matters and being unique in our approach can give rise to feelings of separation and lead to misunderstanding.

Opening the path of an improved version of the world starts with the self. We awaken, and everyone will awaken. We heal, and all will heal. Corrections in our inner world will naturally result in the desired changes around us. So don't worry that we are different; being an independent soul and a disciplined practitioner of alternative paths does not mean we need to be isolated. No one is better than any other. We can love as we always have and come to empathize with our brothers and sisters by viewing them as mere reflections of ourselves.

It is easy to correct the viewpoint that external forces threaten our practices or are against our values because we have already established inner work. Let's be true to our practice for the rest of our journey by upholding the values we have learned so far. Choose to offer patience and empathy as a solution, not superiority and forcible reforms. Seeing with a kind eye and restoring loving-kindness will better serve us emotionally, mentally, and spiritually.

We can all change for the better while remembering that self-directed positive actions are more powerful than wishful thinking, demanding, and wanting without firmness. Do not forget that the origin of power is in the conscious individual within the collective.

Why Practice Together

It is a powerful experience to sit in circles, hold hands, take refuge in each other's arms, rest our heads, and let our hearts open to one another. We cry, play, and laugh with lifelong friends. The loving energy and benefits of practicing together with like-minded souls can help us when we forget the bond we share with other humans. It can feel enriching to restore the profound connection with our teachers, sisters, brothers, fellow practitioners, and friends.

Let's be at home with everyone, restore the once unseen connections, remember what unites and holds us as one, lift what has blinded us, and deepen the profound relationship with all of life. It will serve us all when we come together and offer our presence unconditionally. We can choose to reunite with many of those we lost touch with by showing up as our renewed selves, willing to forgive, understand, and deeply connect.

I encourage all conscious healers to lead and help pave the way for anyone wishing to see the light of healing but facing temporary blindness. It is one of life's purposes for all beings at some point to be students, teachers, and ultimately a guide to seeking souls. We can offer our help or even just an listening ear to anyone near us, including our intimate circle of friends and family members. We can also extend our capacity to include our coworkers, neighbors, and strangers. We can stand next to them as equals and offer a compassionate hand by being a source of hope, inspiration, and motivation through our effortless demonstration and sharing of healthy examples. We can be there for those going through the same human experiences and build a shared practice together.

Why Life Is Waiting

There is no life without healing, but also no healing without the wonders of life. Healing is only possible because we breathe, experience sensations, and have a beating heart. It is meaningful because we are alive, and it is our birthright to do what we desire. The purpose of recovery is to experience the fullness of life, go on adventures, try new things, and be fearless in our playfulness without facing hindrances when possible. There is no use for healing without the willingness to make use of our recovery. Even energy, vitality, spaciousness, and abundance of resources go to waste without practical application and direction toward growth.

Think of healing as an investment for a new home. Imagine making the down payment, sorting through the paperwork, and undertaking the necessary process but never actually enjoying the comforts of our dwelling space. What about the beautiful kitchen, the spacious rooms, the relaxing hot bath, the fruit tree in the garden, the cozy fireplace, and the humans living in that house? All goes to waste and rots away without the will to enjoy and savor the gifts. We don't know what we already have if we don't actively make use of it. It is important to enjoy life, invest money on good-quality things, eat what is delicious, spend time with friends, get together with family, travel, exercise, immerse in a hobby, and live life while healing. So go out there—life is waiting. Take out the new and shiny boat and row it in the direction you desire.

MESSAGE TO FRIENDS

Since the beginning of my YouTube channel, Heal Your Living, my need to share has always been to return to honesty. Building our community within these past years with my fellow practitioners has led to my soul's calling and spiritual work to be a revealer of light, casting away the shadows within. As my duty to partake in the collective, I share methods of uncovering hidden and repressed emotions and traits to reveal our authentic beingness underneath the clutter. All of my sharing, coaching, and creations stem from personal experience of working with my shadows and revealing my traumas.

The past years of sharing my journey through my videos, writing, podcast episodes, and resources have brought out the fearlessness in me. The presence of listeners, friends, and supportive people helped me further cast away the shadows and continue healing my darkness. I no longer desire to return to old habits of hiding underneath falsehood, pretending to be someone else, being aggressively defensive, directing blame elsewhere, and denying my insecurities. I feel free to reveal what is true about myself and my lifestyle, including my imperfections and flaws.

I arrive at each sharing, in front of our community as I naturally transfer my inner beingness, my spiritual core, without filtering to the external world. I reap in fullness the undeniable benefit of living as my simplest self, showing up without layers of deception, and seeing eye to eye, face to face, and human to human with friends. I enjoy fearless honesty more than ever because I know the rewards of deep connection, the infinite source of true unconditional love.

I feel empowered to continue sharing the shy and sensitive side of my anxieties and highly sensitive personality (HSP) traits and the more confident and courageous personalities within me. My heart continues to grow open, revealing the complexity of my human makeup and the endless possibility of birth within the universe. It is a joyous feeling to be light and spacious without much to carry but only to explore, create, and express with all of those in our community.

Thank you, friends. I wish to be of continual service to all as my true self. I send deep gratitude to our community and sangha.

Parallax Press, a nonprofit publisher founded by Zen Master Thich
Nhat Hanh, publishes books and media on the art of mindful living
and Engaged Buddhism. We are committed to offering teachings that
help transform suffering and injustice. Our aspiration is to contribute
to collective insight and awakening, bringing about a more joyful,
healthy, and compassionate society.

View our entire library at parallax.org.